Ten Transforming Truths

Ten
Transforming
Truths

by
David A. Palmer

PLACE TO GROW
PRESS
2021

Printed in the United States of America

First Printing, 2021

ISBN 978-1-7321245-8-5

Place to Grow Press
1435 East Main Street
Kent, OH 44240

www.KentMethodist.org

Contents

Preface

Be transformed by the renewing of your mind.

Romans 12:2

There are truths which – once grasped – transform life. Newton's laws of motion transformed our human understanding of mechanics. The Copernican revolution transformed our whole vision of the cosmos. Einstein's concept of relativity further transformed how we are able to interact with the physical world. These scientific truths are now so widely accepted that few people think about how revolutionary they once were. But their transforming effect continues.

There are religious truths that were likewise revolutionary when they first took hold in the human understanding, and that have been extraordinarily transformational in human life. Some of these truths have so thoroughly shaped our contemporary world that people do not think about how they originated. Yet even as people at times deny religion, they continue to be affected by the fundamental truths that religion has discerned.

Religion has been a part of human life since the beginning of the human race. As far as we can tell, every ancient culture in every place was religious. People have universally had a sense of an Ultimate Reality and have responded to that Reality in acts of worship and ritual. At the same time, the specific religious ideas held by various peoples have been extremely diverse. People have had different concepts of God (or the gods) and different notions about how human beings should relate to the divine and should live with one another. They have had various ideas about our human purpose and destiny. Just as early scientific inquiry developed particular ideas that missed the mark—such as the Ptolemaic model for the universe or the idea that disease was caused by miasma—so early religion produced multiple ideas that we now consider problematic.

Take a visit to Teotihuacan—the great pre-Aztec center near Mexico City—and you will see a prime example of this. On the top of a giant pyramid, the priests of Teotihuacan would cut out the beating hearts of sacrificial victims to offer them to the gods. The victims were typically people who had been captured from neighboring tribes. The people of Teotihuacan were sincere in their thinking—just as Ptolemaic astronomers were sincere—but they surely missed the mark in their search for truth.

In the course of scientific progress, the misguided notions of the past were ultimately judged to be false, as truths emerged which have transformed human life. The same has happened in the history of religion.

The focus of this book will be on ten transforming truths which have come through the Biblical witness. These are truths which have thoroughly transcended ideas of the past and have dramatically transformed the world in which we live today. This will not be an exhaustive survey of all the truths that have ever come through religions everywhere. But these ten particular ideas have been watersheds. To grasp them is to understand the transformative power of religious truth.

Truth is liberating. To know the truth is to be set free for a better life and a brighter future. Truth has power to change life. It is a power well expressed by Jesus when he said, "You will know the Truth, and the Truth will set you free." (John 8:32)

Acknowledgements

A book like this comes into being only with strong support from many directions. I wish to acknowledge:

My wife, Mavis, who puts up with all the time I spend on books like this and supports me no matter what.

United Methodist Church of Kent staff members Adam C. Alderson and Sarah Brosvic, who provided the proofreading and publishing support needed to bring this book, and others like it, into its final printed format.

Rev. Richard Mitchell, retired United Methodist pastor who is a part of the Kent church, who suggested the title, "Ten Transforming Truths."

The congregation of the United Methodist Church of Kent, which offers a wonderful field for ministry and mission.

Above all I give glory to God, whose Spirit is the source of all truth.

The One God Is Good

The Lord our God is One

Deuteronomy 6:4

The Lord is good

Psalm 25:8; 35:8, 100:5; 118:1; 135:3; 145:9

Human beings seem to have a built-in capacity to be aware of God, so much so that scientists have remarked that human beings appear to be hard-wired for God. This natural awareness of God is expressed historically in the fact that religion was at the center of every ancient society. The awareness of the reality of God has continued through the centuries. In America today, a large segment of the population is not active in church, and yet the great majority of those people would still say that they are "spiritual." Human beings have had an abiding sense that there is a spiritual reality that surrounds us; there is a higher power beyond us.

But people have not been so clear when it comes to conceiving what that higher power is like. Most ancient peoples imagined that the higher power is actually a collection of powers—that there are numerous gods—and they imagined those gods to be in conflict with one another. In the ancient Near East, in virtually all cultures from the Babylonians to the Greeks, the gods were typically envisioned as capricious, self-centered, and squabbling—and not overly interested in human beings. The gods might at times control chaos, but they also might at times create chaos. The world was thus seen as an unreliable realm; you could never be sure if the next growing season would come. Religion in this context involved a set of rituals designed to appease the gods, get their attention, and move them into beneficial action.

The gods were not seen as bad, but neither were they seen as good. Ancient near eastern religions would have said rather that the gods *do not care*. The higher powers of the universe blast along without particular concern for human beings.

This world view, in its basic contours, is essentially the world view represented by atheism today. Take out the mythological language about pantheons of squabbling gods, and you have the modern idea that the universe is ruled by a set of cosmic powers that collide together with no moral framework and no regard for human beings.

But out of a tiny religious community in the ancient Near East came a revolutionary message – *The Lord our God is One. (Deuteronomy 6:4)*. The monotheism of the Old Testament was utterly unique in the ancient world. Although the Egyptian Pharaoh Akhenaten briefly promoted the worship of a sole god – the sun disc Aten – his thinking was not well developed, and his ideas were quickly rejected after his death. In sharp contrast, the Hebrew community persistently declared a coherent message that there is a unified power governing the universe. There is one God who reigns over all and holds all things together.

Moreover, the people of Israel declared that this one God is **good**. The affirmation that God is good is one of the most oft-repeated affirmations in the Bible. Over and over the Bible declares that God cares for all creation and beneficently rules over all things. This entire concept of the nature of God – *the one God is good* – proved revolutionary, for it would completely transform how people viewed the universe. As it took hold across the centuries, it ultimately provided the philosophical underpinnings for modern science. The conviction that there is one divine Power, who providentially governs the universe, meant that the world is not fundamentally a chaotic place ruled by capricious gods, but rather it is a reliable realm, with laws established firmly by God, who provides shape and order to all things. This gave people the confidence that they should be able to discern those laws and make dependable discoveries about the structure of the universe.

The affirmation that God is good declares further that this world was created for good purpose. Across the ancient world there was a widespread notion that this world is an inferior, degraded realm, far diminished in comparison to the realm of the gods. Some religions specifically counselled a spiritual withdrawal from the rottenness of the world. But in the creation story in the book of Genesis, every aspect of this world is described with the statement, "God saw that it was good." (Genesis 1) This very positive assessment of creation led over time to the conviction that human beings are meant to be caretakers of this good earth and should share in God's good purposes. The concern today for the environment and the widespread idea that every person should "make the world better" are rooted in the basic conviction that the world is intended to be a good place.

But if the one God is good, and if God intends the world for good, why then is there evil in the world? This was not a pressing question for most ancient cultures. If you asked an ancient Babylonian or Greek why there are bad things in the world, the answer would be, "Because the gods are up to no good." But the question does arise if the central affirmation is that the one God is good. This indeed is a central point at which atheists often object to belief in God, saying, "How can there be a good God when there are so many bad things in the world?"

But if people deny God, they must answer the opposite question: "If there is no God, why do we even have an idea of good and evil?" Human beings universally have a concept of "the good," and there is a strong sense among people that we should "do good." Why is this so? If human beings are simply the random result of physical processes—or the product of uncaring gods—we should not even think in terms of good and evil. We should just be concerned about our own survival and advancement, and we certainly should not have any sort of overarching high ideal of "the good." Even if human beings were naturally kind to their family members and their own tribe, on account of the fact that this would further their own well-being and advancement, the sort of moral ethic that is embodied in Jesus—that one should give of oneself for the sake of the stranger—should appear as completely nonsensical. Yet the high level of goodness exemplified in Jesus resonates within the human heart. Even people who do not "believe" in Jesus affirm his moral ethic. This only makes sense if there is some principle of goodness in the universe—some source of our concept of the good, some spark for our sense that we have an imperative to do good. The affirmation that God is good explains the moral conscience that is within every human being. Our concept of the good is a reflection of the goodness of God.

But if God is good, how then do we explain the evil that makes headlines every day? The saga in the book of Genesis that portrays God as good goes on to explain the problem of evil in the story of Adam and Eve. This story is less about the first human beings and much more about all of us. The story depicts how God creates human beings and blesses them with all that they need. As God places humans within a wonderful world, God gives to the human beings something quite remarkable – the freedom to choose how to live, and even whether or not to follow God. This aspect of the story is extraordinary, especially within the context of the ancient world, where rulers did not grant freedom to their subjects, especially the freedom to disobey the ruler. The ancient idea of kingship was that a proper society would be one in which people were compelled to follow the king. Sometimes today people imagine that God should compel everyone to follow God's will, intervening to stop people if ever they would do wrong. But the story of Adam and Eve contains a deep insight – that a genuinely good world will be one in which people are free to choose how they will live, even if this carries the risk that people will choose poorly; for it is only when people freely choose the good that their goodness will be authentic.

The Biblical idea that *the one God is good* thus entails the realization that a fully good world cannot be a puppet show. It cannot be a realm in which God pulls the strings to control the story line; but it must be a free arena in which moral agents themselves choose to act in goodness. This necessarily allows for the possibility of moral evil—the harm that people do to others—because some people will choose wrongly. It also allows for the possibility of so-called "natural evils"—the pains that are caused by forces of nature—because it is only in a world full of challenges and hard edges that moral choices make a real difference. Genuine goodness will exist in the world not when wrongs and troubles are prevented by God from ever happening, but when evil is overcome with good. This will be the trajectory of the whole Biblical story.

The truth that *the one God is good* thus leads finally to the awareness that we as human beings have a calling to choose the good for ourselves and to do the good in our personal lives. Here is where this truth is most transformational. The conviction that God is good has inspired people to engage in enormous acts of goodness throughout the centuries.

In the early years of Christianity, the most distinctive feature of Christians within the paganism of the Roman Empire was how Christians gave compassionate assistance to people in need. Christians had a welfare program for widows that was without parallel in the ancient world; and they made a particular impression in the second and third centuries when major plagues swept through the empire. As thousands in the cities fell from the plagues, the general response of the population was to stay as far away from the sick and dying as possible. The early bishop Dionysius, who served in Alexandria during the Plague of Cyprian in the mid-third century, described the situation among pagans as follows: "At the first onset of the disease, they pushed the sufferers away and fled from their dearest, throwing them into the roads before they were dead, and treated unburied corpses as dirt, hoping thereby to avert the spread and contagion of the fatal disease; but do what they might, they found it difficult to escape." In contrast, Christians engaged in self-sacrificial care for both Christian and pagan neighbors. As Dionysius reported, "Most Christians showed unbounded love and loyalty.... Heedless of danger, they took charge of the sick, attending to their every need and ministering to them in Christ... The best of our brethren lost their lives in this manner."[1] This extraordinary care on the part of Christians resulted in many more people coming to Christian faith, as they saw the real impact that Christianity made on human behavior.

The general charitable goodness of early Christians was well summarized by the church leader Tertullian (late second to early third centuries), when he described Christian practice as follows: "We do not take gifts and spend them on feasts, drinking-bouts, or fancy restaurants. Instead we use them to support and bury poor people, to supply the needs of boys and girls who have no means and no parents. We support the elderly confined now to their homes. We also help those who have suffered shipwreck. Primarily it is the acts of love that are so noble that lead many to put a brand upon us. "See," they say, "how they love one another."[2]

---

1   Dionysius of Alexandria, quoted in Rodney Stark, <u>The Rise of Christianity</u>.
2   Tertullian, <u>Apology</u>, chapter 39.

People inspired by the goodness of God have continued this pattern of loving deeds into the present day. In modern times, many people have so internalized the truth that we are meant to live in goodness that even if they give no thought to God, they have a feeling that we ought to be doing good. Yet the idea that people should give bountifully of themselves in goodness is not self-evident. It has arisen out of the religious truth that *the one God is good*, and the exchange of that truth for other ideas about reality will logically produce a very different result. If we think, for example, that the powers that govern the universe are uncaring, as many ancient pagans thought, then we are likely to be motivated to just save our own skin—exactly what many pagans did during Roman plagues. If we think that God is bloodthirsty, then we will likely be motivated to sacrifice our enemies, as the people of ancient Teotihuacan did. If we think that God is vengeful and hates "unbelievers," then we will become modern terrorists. It is notable that when radical Islamists commit acts of brutality, they typically shout, "God is great." They never shout, "God is good." It is impossible to hate as they do if one truly believes in God's goodness.

To acknowledge that *the one God is good* changes life. It changes life on an individual level when people recognize that they are in the hands of a good God, and it can change all human society when those people become instruments of goodness in the world.

God Created You in God's Image

In the beginning God created...

Genesis 1:1

God created human beings in the image of God

Genesis 1:27

God formed human beings from the dust of the earth, breathing in them the breath of life

Genesis 2:7

A foundational truth in the Bible explodes forth in the opening words of Genesis: "In the beginning God created." Genesis continues with a grand, poetic account which declares that the whole universe is the intentional, purposeful creation of God, and we as human beings are the pinnacle of God's design, as we have been created in God's image. This is a dramatically different picture from what prevailed in the rest of the ancient Near East.

In all the lands of the ancient Near East, people had a variety of creation myths – stories told to account for the existence of the universe and human beings. The myths had different details but a similar basic outlook. They generally envisioned the world as resulting from a chaotic battle between the gods – a giant conflict between cosmic powers – out of which the world emerged as a kind of unintended consequence. In the ancient Babylonian myth, for example, the earth was thought to be the body of a god who was slain in the conflict. Human beings in this scenario were a further afterthought; they were not considered to be in any sort of noble relationship to God. In the Babylonian myth, the chief god finally created humans to be slaves to the gods, so that lesser gods could be relieved of their duties.

If you look past the mythological language, you can notice the close similarity between the basic outlook of these ancient myths and the way that many people think about the universe today. When people say that the universe is just the unintended result of a chaotic clash of cosmic forces, and that human beings have no special place in the universe, they are voicing the same basic ideas as ancient Babylonians, just dressed up in modern language.

What the Bible proclaims is radically different. Its message was revolutionary in the ancient world and continues to be transformative today. The Biblical vision declares that the universe was intentionally created by God, according to a good design and a grand purpose, with human beings created in a special place. On the one hand, human beings are one with the rest of creation—they are created, says Genesis, "out of the dust of the earth"—but they are also created "in the image of God." This makes a decisive declaration about who you are.

If the ancient and modern myths are true, then you are nobody special. You are here by accident, just a random blob of protoplasm that is soon to be extinguished. The best you can do is to try to manipulate the world around you in order to survive as long as possible, and nothing you do has any real meaning. But the message proclaimed in the opening words of Genesis changes everything. The idea that you are "in the image of God" proclaims that while you are a physical being, you have a spiritual nature, a fundamental kinship with God.

It is notable that the Biblical picture does affirm our physicality and our oneness with the rest of the natural world. In Genesis one, creation is described as occurring through a progressive process—pictured in the imagery of the "days of creation"—which eventually involves the emergence of plants and animals of all kinds and finally human beings. Human beings are grouped with the higher animals on "day six" of the saga. This picture corresponds with modern biology. Human beings in their physical make-up are fully part of the natural order of planet earth.

But while the Biblical saga affirms our commonality with the rest of creation, it also declares that there is something very special about us. The proclamation that we are "in the image of God" points to a set of spiritual qualities that sharply distinguish us from the rest of the natural world. These include the major aspects of who we are.

Like God, human beings **create**. Animals often build things. Squirrels build nests and beavers build dams, which throughout time look pretty much the same. Animals also produce music — birds sing and insects chirp — and like the things that animals build, the songs are always the same and serve a functional purpose. Human beings do something entirely different: they create new things. Like God, they bring into existence designs that did not exist before. Moreover, human beings not only create functional items; they create art. They create purely for the sake of beauty.

Art makes no sense at all if human beings are simply material entities that are the chance result of mechanical forces, as many people want to insist today. If we are merely physical beings that arose out of chaos, out of a dog-eat-dog struggle for existence, we should have no interest in beauty for its own sake; we should only want to do things that advance our survival. Yet we marvel at flowers and snowflakes and we gaze at sunsets, and we devote enormous energy to creating music and painting and sculpture. This makes no sense – until we grasp the message that we are made in the image of God. In the Genesis account, God creates a marvelous world, full of wonder, and when God beholds it "God sees that it is good." (Genesis 1:10,12,18,21,25,31) Human beings reflect the nature of God when they create beauty and appreciate beauty, along with creating a host of marvelous things.

Furthermore, like God, every human being is a **moral agent.** We understand good and evil, we can freely choose to do the good, and we can express authentic love, including the sort of radical self-giving love for unrelated other people such as is exemplified in Jesus. This goes far beyond anything that can be seen in the animal world. While animals naturally show care for their own circle – an important element for survival – we do not find animals pondering moral issues or launching into campaigns to improve the lives of all the rest of the animals on the planet. They simply follow their natural drives. Human beings, in contrast, are "in the image of God" in their ability to consider and carry out wide-ranging loving actions for good.

Along with this, human beings also have the capacity to **comprehend.** We can understand the world, raise questions and explore, and reflect about meaning and purpose. No other creatures on the planet sit around in discussion groups, or establish universities, or develop scientific projects, or write books, or ponder the meaning of life. We are on a completely different level in our ability to critically analyze and comprehend the universe. This again is part of what it means to be "in the image of God."

Of all the distinctive qualities that human beings have, the highest and perhaps most interesting is our **religious sense** – human beings have an awareness of God and regularly respond to God in devotional practices and worship and entire religious systems. The religious sense of human beings is evidenced both in the universality of religion and in the tenacity of religion. During the twentieth century, there were several thoroughgoing, brutal, and extended attempts to stamp out religion – in the Soviet Union, in communist China, and in Cambodia – which were all complete failures. In 1949, when the Communists took over China, there were only about four million Christians, and Mao campaigned harshly for years to eliminate them; but today there are approximately 100 million Christians in China. In Russia, following more than seventy years of state-enforced atheism, the Russian Orthodox Church, along with other denominations, has emerged alive and well. Cambodia again has an official religion enshrined in its constitution – Buddhism – and the Christian community, which was almost completely exterminated by the Khmer Rouge, is growing rapidly. By all appearances, the apostle Paul had it right when he quoted the ancient Greeks and said, "In God we live and move and have our being." (Acts 17:28) There is an ingrained religious sense in human beings that has persisted in every place throughout the ages. This is very difficult to explain, until we recognize the truth in the statement that *we are created in the image of God*. The highest meaning of that statement is that each human being is able to know God and enter into a relationship with God. This suggests that human beings will only find their ultimate fulfillment when they enter into a personal fellowship with God. As St. Augustine put it, "You have created us for Yourself, O God, and our hearts are restless until they find rest in You."[1]

The truth declared in the opening chapter of the Bible – that *God created you in the image of God* – finds its culmination in the apex of the Biblical story, in the coming of Jesus Christ. The New Testament proclaims that divinity becomes united with humanity in Jesus. The Incarnation is the ultimate confirmation of the fundamental connection between God and human beings, and it expresses the intent of God to bring people into harmonious union with God. Human beings may be one with the rest of creation in their physical make-up, but at the same time they are far more. In their fundamental identity they are made to have a profound spiritual bond with God.

The truth that *God created you in the image of God* is transformational when it is accepted, for it comprehensively shapes how you think of yourself and how you think of others. It means that *you are a person of infinite value.* You are not just a temporary creature that has randomly appeared in the universe. You are here because God made you, and you are intended for a relationship with God; thus you are of enormous worth in God's sight. This also means that *you have a purpose in life* – a God-given calling to grow in fellowship with God and to live as a child of God. Many people struggle to find any sort of meaning in existence. But life has tremendous meaning when we understand ourselves to be a part of the eternal design

---

1   Augustine, <u>Confessions</u>.

of God; and our lives make a real difference as we live out that purpose by using our God-given abilities to make an impact on the world around us. Furthermore, the truth that human beings are in the image of God means that *all people are to be treated as God's children.* We cannot disregard, oppress, or exploit others if we truly acknowledge that they are God's people made in God's image. We will perceive rather that we are all intended to value and support and help one another.

The truth that *God created human beings in the image of God* has been transformational in human history; for as it has become accepted, it has provided the philosophical foundation for advances in human rights. If human beings are made in God's image, then it follows that every person should be regarded as equally valuable, and every person must be seen as having the same high standing in God's universe. This perception is reflected in the U.S. Declaration of Independence when it says, "We hold these truths to be self-evident, that all men are created equal, and that they are endowed by their Creator with certain inalienable rights."

Many people will tell you that you are just here by chance, in which case your life finally adds up to nothing. But the transforming truth is that you and your neighbor are here on purpose; we are each a special creation of God, designed to grow in deep fellowship with God and to share together as God's children. To take hold of that truth is to have the foundation for a life that makes sense and a human community that reaches its high calling.

The Problem Is Sin

Now the serpent was more crafty than any other wild animal that the Lord God had made. He said to the woman, "Did God say, 'You shall not eat from any tree in the garden'?" The woman said to the serpent, "We may eat of the fruit of the trees in the garden; but God said, 'You shall not eat of the fruit of the tree that is in the middle of the garden, nor shall you touch it, or you shall die.'" But the serpent said to the woman, "You will not die; for God knows that when you eat of it your eyes will be opened, and you will be like God, knowing good and evil." So when the woman saw that the tree was good for food, and that it was a delight to the eyes, and that the tree was to be desired to make one wise, she took of its fruit and ate; and she also gave some to her husband, who was with her, and he ate. Then the eyes of both were opened, and they knew that they were naked; and they sewed fig leaves together and made loincloths for themselves. They heard the sound of the Lord God walking in the garden at the time of the evening breeze, and the man and his wife hid themselves from the presence of the Lord God among the trees of the garden. But the Lord God called to the man, and said to him, "Where are you?" He said, "I heard the sound of you in the garden, and I was afraid, because I was naked; and I hid myself." He said, "Who told you that you were naked? Have you eaten from the tree of which I commanded you not to eat?" The man said, "The woman whom you gave to be with me, she gave me fruit from the tree, and I ate." Then the Lord God said to the woman, "What is this that you have done?" The woman said, "The serpent tricked me, and I ate."

Genesis 3:1–13

If you go to the doctor because you are suffering from some ailment, you will begin by describing your symptoms, but the doctor will seek to answer the bigger question as to what is causing the symptoms. The key step in healing your ailment will be to correctly *diagnose the problem.*

Human beings suffer from all sorts of ailments. People suffer from anxiety and insecurity. They suffer from conflicts with one another and manifold acts of harming one another and a general lack of peace in the world. They suffer from guilt and sorrow. They suffer from fear about the future, and a lack of meaning and purpose in the present. Human beings wrestle of course with many kinds of physical ailments, but the larger and yet more difficult ailments are the spiritual ones. People sense that they lack wholeness, they perceive that their world is not the way it should be, and they are afflicted with a spiritual malaise.

All these things are symptoms. The key question is: What is the cause; what is the fundamental human problem? Only when we diagnose the problem can we discern the real answer.

When it comes to diagnosis, there are two basic things that can go wrong. Sometimes people will go to the doctor with a set of troublesome symptoms, but in spite the best effort by experts, they can never quite figure out what the problem is. The same happens in human life in general.

People will suffer from a lack of peace and wholeness and well-being, but they never figure out the fundamental problem, and so their troubled condition stays the same.

If you have *no diagnosis* – the real problem remains hidden – you look for things that at least promise in some way to make you feel better. This pattern can be seen in a great deal of human behavior. People will seek entertainments and diversions, or they will use alcohol or drugs, or they will embark on quests after wealth or fame, all in the effort to dull their troubles and make themselves feel better. But such activities, even if temporarily successful, only mask the underlying problem.

The other major way in which diagnosis can go askew is when the *wrong diagnosis* is made. This results in the wrong therapy being applied, which can lead to even more troubles. Within human history, there have been multiple times when people have made the wrong diagnosis of the human problem; and they have consequently come up with the wrong prescription, causing thereby even more troubles. One of the classic examples of this in world history can be seen in the philosophy of Karl Marx, whose philosophy ruled over nearly half the world's population fifty years ago and still persists in places today. Marx said that human beings are economic animals, and their problem is economic disparity – a wealthy class owns the means of production, while the working class slaves away. Religion, he said, is part of the problem, because it supports the status quo. The solution therefore, he declared, is to get rid of the owners and get rid of religion and get rid of property altogether. Once everything became owned by everyone, paradise would soon ensue. The government, he said, would just fade away. People would freely produce and share in the fruits of their common labor and would live in peace and happiness and plenty. For an example of how this theory worked out, one need only look at North Korea today

Marxism was a disaster. Marxist governments did not fade away but became some of the most oppressive and war-mongering in history. The people labored, but productivity was terrible, because there was no incentive to improve processes. Marxist economies became characterized by scarcity rather than plenty, and there was still a division between the haves and have-nots, with the top party members being the haves and the people being the have-nots. Marxism produced the opposite of paradise.

What went wrong? Marx misdiagnosed the human problem, and so made all the wrong prescriptions. He pointed to a human ailment—the sometimes large division between rich and poor, which is also critiqued in the Bible—but he completely misjudged the human condition and missed the real problem, which is much deeper.

The fundamental human problem is a spiritual one. It is correctly diagnosed in the one book that Marx rejected—in the opening pages of the Bible, where it is dramatically addressed and illuminated in the story of Adam and Eve.

The story of Adam and Eve seems on the surface to be a simple one. A man and woman are in a garden, with a tree that has forbidden fruit, and a talking snake, and an unfolding story line that ultimately has God strolling in the garden and the people hiding from God behind the shrubbery. These elements are markers which tell you that you are not supposed to read this story literally! Generally, if you read a story that has talking animals,[1] you know that it is not meant to be read as a historical account; and the same is certainly true with the story of the Garden of Eden. This is not a quaint story about some quirky event that happened in some garden millennia ago. This is an Old Testament parable, which speaks profoundly about our human condition and our human problem.[2]

The first human character in the story does not have a name. Adam in Hebrew is not a name; it is a word that means "human being." "Eve" is a name, but she receives the name at the end of the story; she is designated throughout the story as "the woman." This indicates that the human characters in this story represent everyone. They are not two people who lived in some distant past, upon whom we can place the blame for our current troubles. Adam and Eve are you and me.

---

1   Note that the serpent in Genesis 3 is described as "a wild animal that the Lord God made." (Genesis 3:1) The original Hebrew word for serpent in this verse is *nachash* נָחָשׁ – the basic word for "snake." The snake is later punished by being forced to crawl on its belly (Genesis 3:14). It was later Christians who read the Devil into this story. The story itself consistently portrays the serpent as an animal. The ancient Hebrews were using a figurative story, never meant to be taken literally, to convey spiritual truth.

2   The church theologian Origen spoke in the early third century about how the story is meant to be read figuratively: "When it is said that God walked in the garden in the evening and that Adam hid himself behind a tree, I cannot imagine that anyone will doubt that these details point figuratively to spiritual meanings, using a narrative which has a semblance of history but which did not literally happen." De Principiis IV, 1.6.

They are created by God and placed in a wonderful world. God blesses them with all that they need, and they in response are called to be obedient and faithful to God. This is represented in the story in the fact that they are given the fruit of many trees to eat, and at the same time they are commanded to not eat the fruit of one particular tree. But temptation slithers in – in the form of the snake. The heart of the temptation is posed in the story in the words of the serpent: "If you eat the fruit of this tree, you will be like God." (Genesis 3:5) The woman and the man take the fruit and eat.

Here is the essence of what the Bible will call "sin." Sin is putting ourselves in the place of God – deciding that we will call the shots and we will go our own way, no matter what God says. Sin is the breach between human beings and God, which then results in division and blaming and fighting and misery among human beings. In the story, the man blames the woman for giving him the apple to eat; she blames the snake. The fighting gets worse in the next story, where Cain kills his brother Abel.

In sin human beings try to exalt themselves – to be "like God" in the sense of trying to be on a level with God – but they end up in disorder and instability and discover that they are in fact weak and vulnerable. In the story, the man and the woman after disobeying God discover that they are naked. This does not mean that they discover their sexuality. It is much earlier in the Genesis account that they are told to "be fruitful and multiply" (Genesis 1:28); so they are already quite aware of their sexuality. What they discover is their vulnerability—that they are exposed to danger and trouble. So they hide, because they are afraid.

The story is a striking picture of our human condition—how in alienation from God we end up in fear, hiding ourselves from God, distrusting one another. Ultimately, human beings try to answer their weakness by looking for sources of strength and salvation around them, and they end up putting their trust in all kinds of false gods, such as money or power or political systems; but none of it brings deliverance.

In all this, the story of Adam and Eve makes clear what our fundamental human problem is. *The problem is sin—our alienation from God—*which then results in the self-centeredness and fighting, the emptiness and anxiety, the exploitation of others, the abuse of the planet, and the many kinds of foolishness that one sees in the world today. The answer will be for human beings to somehow come back into a real connection and a right relationship with God.

If Karl Marx had realized that the human problem is sin, he would have known that even if you kill off all the owners and give the property to the state, you will have solved nothing, because the new rulers will still be caught up in the quest for power, people will still be self-centered and won't want to work hard if it only benefits others, and people will still suffer from a deep spiritual malaise, because they are far more than the economic animals that Marx supposed them to be. Marxism failed, as many human philosophies have, because it did not grasp the human problem.

The human problem is a spiritual one. The answer must therefore address the fundamental spiritual breach that human beings cause in every generation – the way in which people become alienated from God, from one another, and from their own true selves.

But once a proper diagnosis is made, the further major question arises: "Is there a remedy?" The human problem is not easily corrected. In the history of religion, people have often gained insight into the human problem, but many attempted remedies have fallen short. The real answer to the problem will be the subject of the next chapter.

God Acts to Save

"The Lord says, 'Before they call, I will answer.'"

Isaiah 65:24

God shows His love for us in that while we were yet sinners, Christ died for us.

Romans 5:8

God put forth Christ as an atonement for sin … effective through faith.

Romans 3:25

In Christ God was reconciling the world to himself.

II Corinthians 5:19

On January 26, 2016, the Modern Express cargo ship, on its way toward La Havre, France, foundered in the Bay of Biscay, 130 miles west of Spain. In rough seas and strong winds, it listed to a forty-degree angle. Without power and sharply askew, it was driven by the current toward a potential crash point somewhere along the coast of France. There were twenty-two sailors on the ship.

The predicament of those sailors forms an apt illustration of our human condition. We embark into life with an impressive set of abilities. The crew with that ship could transport massive loads across great distance; and in human life generally, we are all able, with our God-given gifts of reason and moral discernment and various talents, to accomplish marvelous things. But like the ship, we get into trouble. We fall into sin—we ignore God and go our own way and cut ourselves off from God—and our human life in consequence becomes sharply askew. We slide into damaging behaviors and misplaced priorities and distorted values. Off-kilter and adrift, we end up driven inexorably toward destruction.

But we are not alone on the seas of life. The Modern Express sent a distress signal, which was picked up by Salvamento Maritimo, the Spanish search and rescue agency, which sent two rescue helicopters; a salvage ship was also dispatched. The helicopters airlifted the sailors off the ship, one by one, until all twenty-two had been brought to safety. Meanwhile, the salvage tug labored to attach a tow line to the Modern Express, which was quite difficult in heavy seas, but the effort was finally successful at a point when the Modern Express was just 26 nautical miles from running aground. The ship was towed to safe harbor.

The twenty-two sailors on that listing ship were keenly aware of one reality: they needed salvation. They might have tried to save themselves—they could have looked for some oars or tried to hoist a sail—but such efforts would have been woefully inadequate and futile. On the other hand, they could have simply resigned themselves to their fate and opened the liquor cabinet, dulling their senses in a party until they crashed into oblivion. Instead, the sailors looked for rescue, which came.

Precisely this step of looking to a "higher power" is often lacking in human life. People may readily acknowledge that human life is off kilter and that we are all in peril, but they often wish to imagine that we can somehow straighten things out on our own. Yet to think that we do not need salvation is to seriously underestimate our situation. A survey of human history shows that we are routinely crashing into the rocks, and without any salvation we are each certain to end our own journey in death. Alternatively, people sometimes recognize the grave dilemma in our human situation and just resign themselves to it, with a philosophy which says that we should try to have as good a time as possible before our inevitable ruin. This approach may seem entertaining for a while, but it always results in despair. What transforms our human situation is when we look to a higher power. Talk to anyone involved in

Alcoholics Anonymous or Narcotics Anonymous, and you will hear a personal testimony about that!

In the history of religion, there has been a broad recognition that human life is off kilter and that something needs to happen in order to set things aright. But there have been multiple approaches in the history of religion with respect to what human beings should do. The differing approaches correspond in a way to the possible courses of action for the sailors on that ship.

One of the popular approaches in religion has been the idea that salvation will be achieved through our own rigorous effort. Through self-discipline and self-purification and spiritual practices and moral exertion, one could set one's own life aright, it is hoped, and perhaps have a good impact on the world at large. This pattern has been broadly evident in many world religions. It is especially prominent in some forms of Buddhism and Jainism, and it can be seen in multiple religious movements which have stressed everything that you must do in order to achieve salvation. It is essentially the religious version of the secular idea that we have to somehow save ourselves. The flaw in the whole approach is the reality of sin. In our alienation and weakness, we are not actually in a position to save ourselves. Given our human problem, self-rescue becomes impossible.

An alternative approach in the history of religion and philosophy is to simply give up on the salvation effort and resign oneself to our gloomy destiny. This was the approach of the Stoics in ancient Greece, who said you must courageously accept your fate; or along with that there was the approach of the Epicureans, who said that you might as well party and have as much fun as possible while accepting your fate. Again there are modern secular parallels to these ideas, but this path does not have a happy end.

For the sailors on the Modern Express, the key realization was that there was salvation available from an outside power; and this is a fundamental realization that the Biblical witness seeks to awaken with us—that we will find the answer to our need in a saving Power beyond ourselves. Within the history of religion, there have been multiple points where people have perceived some measure of this truth. People have sensed a need for divine help and have looked for rescue from divine powers. But there have been problems in this approach as well. Typically, in religions across the ancient world, people felt they had to somehow get the attention of disinterested divine powers and curry their favor. This was the purpose of religious ritual in many ancient religions—to try to spur favorable action from the gods. But if this is our situation, there is serious question as to what sort of help we can expect, or whether we can count on any help at all.

Within this entire context, the Biblical message is revolutionary, as it declares that *God acts to save.* The God who has created all things, who is good, and who reigns over all things is acting on our behalf, in order to save us. God, according to the Biblical witness, does not need to be spurred into action; *God takes the initiative.* In the case of the Modern Express, the sailors at least had to put out an S.O.S.; but the Bible declares that God reaches to human beings with saving help even before they call. As Isaiah proclaimed, "The Lord says, 'Before they call, I will answer.'" (Isaiah 65:24) The ultimate example of this in the Biblical story is the coming of Jesus Christ. Jesus' birth is on God's initiative; and Jesus gives himself for humanity even though people at the time are rejecting him. The apostle Paul put it succinctly: "God shows His love for us in that while we were yet sinners, Christ died for us." (Romans 5:8)

But if God is reaching to humanity, human beings will find rescue only if they can finally become connected to God's saving action. On the Modern Express, the sailors were rescued as they literally grabbed onto a line that was being dropped to them from the helicopter. The ship was likewise rescued when it became attached to a line extended from the salvage ship. In theological terms, the word that describes this process of making a saving connection is the word "atonement." The word can be understood as "at-one-ment." It is the action that will bridge the gap between the sinner who is sinking and God who has the power to save.

Because human beings have themselves turned from God and disregarded God's ways, atonement for us must somehow address the brokenness that we have created and all the wrong that has ensued. This is precisely what Christ does on the cross. He takes all our brokenness and wrong upon himself; and thus Paul says that "God put forth Christ as an atonement." (Romans 3:25) As Christ gives his life on our behalf, he bridges the gap between sinful humanity and God, and he thereby enables us to be forgiven and brought into genuine fellowship with God. The breach between humanity and God is overcome. As Paul put it, "in Christ God was reconciling the world to himself." (II Corinthians 5:19)

To follow the Modern Express illustration, the atonement of Christ is the line of salvation being extended to us. But in order for us to be saved, we need finally to take hold of the line! This is what it means to have *faith*. Paul thus says that "God put forth Christ as an atonement ... effective through faith." (Romans 3:25) Faith is our response of receiving the saving action of God.

Faith is more than belief. There is a commonly held notion today that human beings will be saved by believing that Jesus is the Son of God and Savior. But this is the same as saying that the sailors would have been saved by believing that there was a helicopter overhead. It is surely important to recognize and acknowledge that salvation is at hand; but for the sailors, salvation actually happened as they each made a connection with the line that was extended and trusted in its power to lift them up. Faith is this kind of connection with the saving power of God, extended to us in Christ. It means trusting in Christ to lift us out of our trouble into life.

Moreover, the sailors were saved not only in the moment that they were lifted off the deck, but through the whole journey by which they were brought to safety on land. Sometimes people will say that they were "saved" on a particular day and time. They are identifying the moment when they first put their trust in Christ. But faith actually involves a whole journey; it entails embarking on a journey with Christ. This is why Jesus asked his first disciples not simply to "believe" in him but to *follow* him. "Follow me," Jesus said; and the Scripture continues, "They left their nets and followed him." (Matthew 4:19–20)

If the fundamental human problem is our alienation from God, resulting in all sorts of negative behaviors and traumas, then the solution must involve a major movement of the soul, by which a person comes anew into ongoing harmony with God. This movement is possible because *God acts to save* – reaching with deliverance to human beings who are foundering on rough seas – and the movement becomes complete as people respond in faith, committing themselves with trust into God's saving power.

In all this, it becomes clear that salvation is a gift, which is far beyond what human beings can ever deserve or earn. For the sailors on the Modern Express, rescue arrived without any payment on their part (though perhaps the shipowner had a bill in the end!). God's salvation likewise comes to humanity, as the Scripture says, as a "free gift." (Romans 5:15, 6:23) The full nature of God's generosity will be explored in the next chapter.

For anyone who is stuck in serious trouble, it is a transforming moment to realize that salvation is at hand. The transforming truth proclaimed at the center of the Biblical witness is that salvation is indeed at hand – *God is acting to save*. This is why this truth is often called "good news."

God Acts in Grace

Since all have sinned and fall short of the glory of God, they are now set right with God by his grace as a gift, through the redemption that is in Christ Jesus.

Romans 3:23–24

By grace you have been saved through faith, and this is not your own doing; it is a gift of God.

Ephesians 2:8

The free gift of God is eternal life in Christ Jesus our Lord.

Romans 6:23

Jesus said, "The kingdom of heaven is like a land-owner who went out early in the morning to hire laborers for his vineyard. After agreeing with the laborers for the usual daily wage, he sent them into his vineyard. When he went out about nine o'clock, he saw others standing idle in the marketplace; and he said to them, 'You also go into the vineyard, and I will pay you whatever is right.' So they went. When he went out again about noon and about three o'clock, he did the same. And about five o'clock he went out and found others standing around; and he said to them, 'Why are you standing here idle all day?' They said to him, 'Because no one has hired us.' He said to them, 'You also go into the vineyard.' When evening came, the owner of the vineyard said to his manager, 'Call the laborers and give them their pay, beginning with the last and then going to the first.' When those hired about five o'clock came, each of them received the usual daily wage. Now when the first came, they thought they would receive more; but each of them also received the usual daily wage. And when they received it, they grumbled against the landowner, saying, 'These last worked only one hour, and you have made them equal to us who have borne the burden of the day and the scorching heat.' But he replied to one of them, 'Friend, I am doing you no wrong; did you not agree with me for the usual daily wage? Take what belongs to you and go; I choose to give to this last the same as I give to you. Am I not allowed to do what I choose with what belongs to me? Or are you envious because I am generous?'"

Matthew 20:1–15

s life fair? Many people complain that life is not fair.

The idea of fairness originates early in life, when as children we struggle over who gets what. We complete with other children over toys on the playground. We stress over how much ice cream we get in our bowl. The idea of fairness is a way of controlling the distribution of good things. I am OK with what I get, as long as everyone gets equal time in the sandbox, and as long as my sister does not get more marshmallows in her hot chocolate than I do. The notion of fairness arises out of the desire for self-protection. It is a way of ensuring a claim to a fair share. This is why the most common complaint heard from children is the phrase, "It's not fair!" They say this whenever they feel they are not getting their due.

In the development of human religious ideas through the centuries, one of the most common concepts to emerge has been the idea that God is, or should be, fair. God in the human imagination becomes the heavenly parent who is responsible for seeing that everyone gets an equal share of marshmallows; and if people do not seem to be getting an equal share of marshmallows, there must be some way that God is going to set things straight in the end. Many of the world's religions have this kind of concept built into them. In Hinduism there is the notion of karma, which says that everyone ultimately gets a cosmic payback for everything they do. In Islam there is a concept of final judgment, which says that everyone in the end will get the punishment or the reward that is his or her due. Religions commonly want to say that God is fair, while conversely, atheists will often deny God because it seems to them that the world is not fair.

It is precisely at this point that the Biblical narrative declares one of its most revolutionary ideas. In the Bible, there are many words used to describe the nature of God—good, just, compassionate, mighty—but the Bible never says that God is fair. This is because the notion of fairness arises not from God but from our human sinfulness—our desire to exalt and advance ourselves and protect our own share. According to the Bible, God is not fair. God is not the divine arbiter who must give all people their due. God is far *more* than fair. The word that the Bible uses in this regard to describe God is the word "grace."

"Grace" means giving people what they do not deserve. It means rewarding people with what they have not earned, bestowing upon them far more than their fair share. Grace is unmerited beneficence. When God forgives people who are guilty, and blesses people who are unworthy, that is grace.

The whole story of the Old Testament is a story of God's amazing grace. Abraham does nothing to deserve God's blessing, but God gives him amazing promises. His descendants in Egypt do not show much faith, but God rescues them and leads them to the promised land. In the promised land, the people continually forget God and break God's laws, but God continues to love and guide them. The people do not deserve what God gives; but God is wondrously good to them anyway. God is gracious.

Nevertheless, people in ancient times struggled to grasp the whole idea of God's grace. By the New Testament period, the prevailing idea in popular religion in Palestine was the idea of fairness — that everybody should be receiving their appropriate reward or punishment. In this context, the message of Jesus was stunning, because Jesus fully represented the whole idea of grace.

Jesus' teaching is prominently illustrated in the parable of the workers in the vineyard. In this story, a landowner goes into town early in the morning, presumably about daybreak, to hire day laborers for his vineyard. This was a common scenario in the ancient world, as landowners needed extra hands at certain seasons of the year. If you were a worker needing employment, and if you were industrious, you would be sure to get yourself to the town square at the crack of dawn, so as to have the best chance of getting hired. In the parable, the landowner hires the laborers that he finds in the marketplace and agrees to pay them "the usual daily wage." The original Greek word here is denarius — a coin that represented the standard day's wage for a laborer. A few hours later in the morning, the landowner goes into town again and hires more workers, and he promises to pay the new workers "whatever is right." One would naturally presume that this would be some percentage of the usual daily wage, since a full day's farm work started at dawn. The scenario repeats itself all day long. The landowner goes into town again at noon, and then at 3:00, hiring workers each time. Finally, he goes into town at 5:00 and finds others standing around, and he says to them, "Why are you standing here idle all day?" They say, "Because no one hired us."

The original hearers of the parable would certainly have thought, "Of course no one hired you. You were lazy and did not get yourself to the marketplace until way late. This guy has been hiring all day!" But, says Jesus, "The land-owner said to them, 'You also go into the vineyard.'"

Finally it is pay time. The landowner instructs his manager to hand out the pay starting with the last and ending with the first. The early bird workers naturally assume that those lazybones who came late in the day will be paid some small fraction of the usual daily wage. But when the workers who started at 5:00 get paid, they are given the full daily wage! The workers who came at dawn are now thinking, "Wow, if they got paid the usual daily wage, we should be getting a very nice paycheck!" But when the paymaster gets to them—after they have waited for everyone else to get paid—they receive the usual daily wage. What do they say? It's not fair! Or as Jesus put it, "They grumbled against the landowner, saying, 'These last worked only one hour, and you have made them equal to us who have borne the burden of the day and the scorching heat!'" (Matthew 20:11)

This parable often causes great consternation among modern readers. Clearly, it seems to people, those who were slackers should be rewarded far less than those people who worked long and hard. What happens in the parable is not fair. But this is exactly Jesus' point. God, like the landowner, is not fair. God is far more than fair.

The first workers in the story are not cheated. They receive precisely what they were promised and what they thought at the outset was fair – the usual daily wage. What makes them unhappy, of course, is that the last workers get far more than what they deserved – getting a full day's wage for only an hour's work. But the landowner replies to them, "Friend, I am doing you no wrong. Did you not agree with me for the usual daily wage? Take what belongs to you and go; I choose to give to the last the same as I give to you. Am I not allowed to do what I choose with what belongs to me? Or are you envious because I am generous?" (Matthew 20:13-15)

The landowner is a picture of grace. He pays to the last workers far more than what they deserve. Their pay derives not from what they have earned but from the owner of the vineyard's generosity.

Jesus is telling us that God is like this. God gives us far more than what we deserve. What exactly have we earned in life? God gave us life to begin with. God gave us all our natural abilities. God gave us this marvelous world. We did not earn any of that. And what have we done with all that God has given us? We may have done some good, and some of us may have done more good than others, which leads us to imagine that we should be rewarded more; but the reality is that when it comes to how well we have worked in God's vineyard, we all come up short. As the apostle Paul said, "All have sinned and fall short of the glory of God." (Romans 3:23) We never earned this life to begin with, and we certainly have not earned eternal life. Indeed, with the many good things we have received in the course of this life, we have already been paid far more than what we deserve.

But God chooses to act with extraordinary generosity. God bestows unmerited favor upon human beings, and this gracious activity comes to its culmination as God acts to save us through Jesus Christ. All that God does through Jesus – as Jesus comes to us, joins with us, and gives his life for us – is completely undeserved by us. But God in Christ provides abundantly for our redemption, purely as a free gift. As Paul said in Romans, "They are now set right with God by his grace as a gift, through the redemption that is in Christ Jesus." (Romans 3:24)

This core proclamation of the Bible – that salvation comes by grace – is one of the most revolutionary spiritual ideas in the history of humanity. Even within the history of Christianity, people often have had a hard time with it. At many points through the centuries, Christians have drifted back to the notion that we all should get what we deserve. In the late Middle Ages, for example, the common notion was that the way to overcome the human alienation from God was to work hard enough and become good enough so as to merit God's blessing. This made religion into a toilsome undertaking, in which people perpetually and rightfully felt that they did not measure up.

Transformation came when a German monk named Martin Luther, who tried as hard as anyone to live a meritorious life, realized that he could never rise to God's perfection. His life changed dramatically when he hit upon the Biblical truth about grace. The teaching in Ephesians 2:8 – *by grace you are saved through faith, and this is not your own doing; it is the gift of God*—became the heart of the Protestant Reformation. The Reformation brought people afresh to the realization that the gap between humanity and God is bridged by God's grace.

Accepting the truth about grace is a key step in accepting God's saving action in Jesus. If we think that God will bless us only to the extent that we are worthy, we will never perceive that the way to God's eternal blessing is open right now through Christ. The message that "by grace you are saved" stirs us to recognize that salvation is at hand.

The good news is that God is not fair. If God were fair—if God gave us for eternity exactly what we deserve—we would be in trouble. But the truth that *God acts in grace* declares that God is giving us through Christ infinitely more than we could ever deserve. It is in recognizing that truth that we can be inspired to receive the gift of God's saving grace with joyous faith.

But if God will bless us abundantly in spite of what we deserve, does this then mean that we need not bother trying to do anything good in life? Why not be like the laborers who came at the last hour to the vineyard? If salvation is by grace through faith, it seems that one could just intentionally disregard God and goodness throughout life, with a plan to come to faith at the last moment. The problem with this plan is not only that the "last moment" may come quite by surprise, but even more that having faith makes life much better right now! Having faith enables us to share in God's full blessing in the here and now; and the goodness that ensues in our life is not a burdensome duty we must perform but the outgrowth of the fellowship we share with God.

The truth that *God acts in grace* changes the entire function of "doing good" in the spiritual life. When God is perceived as "fair" – rewarding people precisely according to what each has done – then acts of goodness become the merits we must produce in order to achieve the maximum reward. With this perspective, the spiritual life is laborious and the final reward uncertain. Good deeds are the things one must do in order to receive God's blessing. But when God is recognized as gracious, the whole scenario is transformed. Good deeds are now what we are inspired and empowered to do because God already blesses us with abundant goodness and infinite promise. Our goodness is a response to God's blessing, not a precondition of it. This imparts a joyous freedom to the spiritual life and an authenticity to our acts of goodness. Grounded in God's grace, we do good not in order to earn some reward for ourselves but as a grateful response to all that God has done for us.

But how do we know what "the good" actually is, and how are we enabled to fully do it? This will be the subject of the following chapter.

God Leads Us into What Is Right

God leads the humble in what is right and teaches them God's way.

Psalm 25:9

"This is the covenant I will make with the people in those days," declares the Lord. "I will put my law in their minds and I will write it on their hearts."

Jeremiah 31:33

Can people be good without God? Some people today claim that we do not need God or faith or churches. Human beings, they say, can live perfectly good lives without religion at all. In fact, religion seems at times to cause people to do bad things. This is certainly evident in the religious terrorism that has occurred in parts of the world. Is it possible for human beings to do better without religion?

If you study human cultures, you quickly realize that there is among human beings a universal idea of the good. Not only is it the case that everyone everywhere has a sense of right and wrong, but everyone everywhere agrees on many of the specifics about what exactly is right and what is wrong. For example, there is universal human agreement on the sixth commandment of the ten commandments – thou shalt not murder[1] (as it is expressed literally in the Hebrew) – and there is also agreement on the seventh commandment against adultery and the eighth commandment against stealing and the ninth commandment against dishonesty. There is broad agreement on some form of the "golden rule" – that we should do unto

---

1   Protestant and Orthodox Christians consider this the sixth commandment. Catholics consider it the fifth. The Bible does not actually number the commandments, so while it is clear what the commandments in total are, there are differing interpretations with regard to how to specifically number them.

others as we would wish them to do unto us.[2] There is a kind of *universal moral law,* a highly developed sense of right and wrong that we find in everyone. As noted in chapter one, this detailed moral awareness points clearly to the reality of God, who is the Source of our concepts of the good.

But there is also another force at work among human beings—our tendency to fall into sin. As noted in chapter three, the story of Adam and Eve serves as the prime Biblical illustration of the nature of sin—that sin is the attempt to be "like God," not like God in goodness, but like God in power. In the story, the fundamental temptation is, "If you eat the fruit of this tree, you will be like God, knowing good and evil." (Genesis 3:5) The latter part of this verse is often misunderstood, as people want to take it to mean that Adam and Eve did not understand good and evil until they disobeyed God. But that makes no sense, since in the story they obviously knew before the temptation that it would be wrong to disobey God and it would be right to follow God. The Biblical picture is that people are created by God with a built-in awareness of right and wrong. The Genesis verse makes sense when we realize that the original Hebrew translated as "knowing good and evil" means "to discern what is good and what is evil" and also "to participate in good or evil." In other words, the basic temptation is to make ourselves like God in the sense that we decide what is good or evil—we are the ones in charge—and we choose to follow our own will, disregarding God.

---

2   See Jeffrey Wattles, <u>The Golden Rule</u>, 1996.

There is thus a fundamental tension between our God-given sense of what is right and our sinful tendency to go our own way contrary to God. The moral awareness that comes to us from God very often becomes filtered through our own sinful tendencies, so that what emerges in the end is a distorted morality that is fitted to our own preferences. The result is that even as people may know deep down what is right, they often choose to do what is wrong, and at least for a while may convince themselves that what they are doing is not wrong after all.

There are a variety of ways in which people will water down or twist the sense of right and wrong that God gives us. One of the most common approaches is to acknowledge God-given principles of right living but then to narrow the field as to how they apply. Consider, for example, the interesting history of what people have done with the widely recognized principle: "Thou shalt not murder."

Everyone agrees with this basic principle, but to whom does it apply? Human beings through the ages have repeatedly wanted to narrow the field to which this principle refers. Many peoples have lived by principle, "You shall not kill anyone in your own clan," or "You shall not kill anyone in your own tribe." Later people adopted the principle, "You shall not kill anyone in your own nation," or "You shall not kill anyone in your own religion." In these contexts, it became perfectly all right to kill the clan over the hill or the tribe across the river or that other nation or that other religion. People have routinely convinced themselves that other peoples are somehow less than truly human and not worthy of moral treatment, and the reason they convince themselves of that is because in their sinfulness they want to exalt themselves over those others. They thus shrink the neighborhood when it comes to who qualifies as a neighbor. Islamic State terrorists shrunk their neighborhood very small.

Jesus met this age-old human tendency head-on. Once, after Jesus had said that the greatest commandments are to love God and to love our neighbor, a man asked him, "Who is my neighbor?" (Luke 10:29) Jesus in response told the parable of the good Samaritan. This parable often is not fully understood. People typically imagine that it is about helping other people in their need. It is in part about that, but the full message is grasped only when we understand the characters in the story. Jesus told this parable to a group of Jews, so when he described a man on his way from Jerusalem to Jericho, they naturally pictured this man as a fellow Jew. In the story, the man is beaten by robbers and left badly injured by the side of the road. The first two people who come along are a priest and a Levite—fellow Jews! But they ignore him. Then along comes a Samaritan. The Samaritans were the descendants of people from the northern kingdom of Israel who, centuries before, had intermarried with foreigners and produced a culture which, in Jewish eyes, was of mixed race and adulterated religion. In the first century, Jews despised Samaritans, and Samaritans likewise resented and despised Jews. To grasp the impact of this parable, you have to imagine the Samaritan as being someone from a group that you intensely dislike.

The Samaritan stops. He helps the Jewish man, binding up his wounds and taking him to an inn, where he pays for his stay. Jesus portrays the hated Samaritan as the hero of the story! Jesus concludes the parable by asking, "Which one proved the neighbor?" The man who had started the conversation could not even choke out the word "Samaritan," but rather said, "The one who showed mercy." Jesus replies, "Go and do likewise." (Luke 10:37)

The parable is all about reaching across barriers of distrust, showing compassion to someone from another ethnic group and another religion, and overcoming age-old hatreds. The parable expands our neighborhood to include everyone. Jesus hammered the point home elsewhere in the Sermon on the Mount when he said, "Love your enemies." (Matthew 5:44)

We see the same pattern in all of Jesus' moral teachings – that while human beings perpetually want to lower the bar when it comes to what is called for in moral living (in order to come up with a morality to their own liking), Jesus raises the bar. Jesus expands the picture of morality to the full and real measure of what is good. People in Jesus' day wanted to think that following a decent, law-abiding life was the measure of goodness; Jesus called them to give of themselves to the poor, to the sick, and to the outcast. People wanted to think that throwing a bit of what they had in the temple offering was an adequate measure of giving; Jesus pointed to a woman who gave all of what she had. People wanted to think that they could limit their help to those who were worthy of it; Jesus called people to forgive and embrace even those who had seriously sinned.

In all this it becomes clear why human beings will never achieve authentic goodness on their own. It is because our human sinfulness clouds and distorts our vision of what is good. We may have a God-given capacity to recognize right and wrong, but in our sinfulness we continually want to truncate and manipulate all the principles of morality so as to fit our preferences and our desires. We end up following our own definition of goodness, which is far less than what we are called to be.

Historically, this has at times resulted in various societies and subcultures adopting codes of values that were far less than the Biblical vision. Mafia families have a code of values in which "the good" is whatever advances the family. The Nazis had a code of values in which "the good" was whatever advanced the "master race." Drug gangs have codes of values which prescribe various behaviors that will contribute to the success of the gang. When people say that they can be "good" without God, one must ask the question, "What do you mean by 'good'?" The reality is that without God, there is no reason to necessarily declare one set of values to be preferable to another.

Even if people have a higher ideal of goodness, without God they still struggle with the limitations of our sinful human condition. On the basis of Biblical understanding, it is certainly possible for people who do not believe in God to live out some degree of real goodness, even a high level of goodness, by simply following the sense of "the good" that God has implanted in their hearts. In that case, they are not actually "being good without God;" they are acting on the moral awareness and the moral capacity that

God has imparted to them. But at the same time, no matter how nobly they strive, they are inherently affected by the blurred moral vision and the distorted priorities and the weak resolve that are part of our human sinfulness. Thus Jesus could definitively proclaim, "No one is good but God alone." (Mark 10:18)

Clearly, if human beings are to be able to live in the greatest possible goodness, they need a spiritual transformation, which will enable them both to recognize and to abide in the authentic goodness of God. The path to this transformation is described in the Scriptures.

In the early part of the Old Testament, there is accent on the idea that *God shows people what is good.* God reveals God's commandments, making clear the central principles by which people should live. When the Psalmist says, "Show me, O Lord, your ways" (Psalm 25:4), this is pointing to the concept that God will reveal what is truly good. God does this throughout the Scriptures, and this revelation comes finally to its culmination in Jesus Christ. In Jesus' character and in all of Jesus' actions, he provides the perfect picture of what it means to live a good life.

Furthermore, the Biblical witness makes clear that God not only provides an outward picture of what is good—through the laws of the Old Testament and the example of Jesus—*God imparts an inner guidance into the good.* As noted above, God does this in a broad way by giving to everyone an inward moral awareness; but for those who are open to God in faith, God's direction can expand into a dynamic inner guidance into what is good. The prophet Jeremiah spoke of this when he said that God "would write his law in our hearts" (Jeremiah 33:33); and this concept came to its fulfillment in the New Testament days in the coming of the Holy Spirit. The Holy Spirit is the presence of God within us, to enlighten our minds, to guide us into what is right, and to empower us for living in genuine goodness. As it is said in the second letter of Peter, "His divine power gives us everything needed for life and godliness ... so that you may escape from the corruption that is in the world and may become participants in the divine nature." (II Peter 1:3-4) The promise of the Spirit means that God will give us not only outward instruction but inward inspiration.

Most crucially, *God frees us for goodness by lifting us from sin into grace.* As we are reconciled to God through Christ, we are no longer bound to all those ways in which our sinful condition always distorts our moral thinking and twists our actions. Although we will remain imperfect, through Christ we can know ourselves to be forgiven, and in grace-filled fellowship with God we are enabled finally to move forward in moral living—toward the authentic goodness into which God would lead us.

Human beings know that they ought to be good; but the sad reality is that people fall well short of even their own ideals, and the world as a result is a mess. The transforming truth is that *God leads us into what is right.* There can indeed be a greater goodness in our lives and in our world. It can happen when we respond in faith to God; for then we will more fully know what is good, and we will have the inspiration and the guidance and the empowerment of God to carry out the good in our world. As the Psalmist said, "God leads the humble in what is right." (Psalm 25:9)

Lowliness Is the Path to Godliness

Let the same mind be in you that was in Christ Jesus, who, though he was in the form of God, did not regard equality with God as something to be grasped, but he emptied himself, taking the form of a servant, being born in human likeness. And being found in human form, he humbled himself and became obedient to the point of death – even death on a cross. Therefore God also highly exalted him and gave him the name that is above every name, so that at the name of Jesus every knee should bow and every tongue confess that Jesus Christ is Lord.

Philippians 2:5–11

At that time the disciples came to Jesus and asked, "Who is the greatest in the kingdom of heaven?" He called a child, whom he put among them, and said, "Truly I tell you, unless you change and become like children, you will never enter the kingdom of heaven. Whoever becomes humble like this child is the greatest in the kingdom of heaven."

Matthew 18:1–4

James and John, the sons of Zebedee, came forward to him and said to him, "Teacher, we want you to do for us whatever we ask of you." And he said to them, "What is it you want me to do for you?" And they said to him, "Grant us to sit, one at your right hand and one at your left, in your glory." But Jesus said to them, "You do not know what you are asking. Are you able to drink the cup that I drink, or be baptized with the baptism that I am baptized with?" They replied, "We are able." Then Jesus said to them, "The cup that I drink you will drink; and with the baptism with which I am baptized, you will be baptized; but to sit at my right hand or at my left is not mine to grant, but it is for those for whom it has been prepared." When the ten heard this, they began to be angry with James and John. So Jesus called them and said to them, "You know that among the Gentiles those whom they recognize as their rulers lord it over them, and their great ones are tyrants over them. But it is not so among you; but whoever wishes to become great among you must be your servant, and whoever wishes to be first among you must be slave of all. For the Son of Man came not to be served but to serve, and to give his life a ransom for many."

Mark 10:35–45

Those who exalt themselves will be humbled, and those who humble themselves will be exalted.

Matthew 23:12

I made great works; I built houses and planted vineyards for myself. I made myself gardens and parks, and planted in them all kinds of fruit trees. I made myself pools from which to water the forest of growing trees. I also had great possessions of herds and flocks, and gathered for myself silver and gold. So I became great and surpassed all who were before me in Jerusalem ... Then I considered all that my hands had done and the toil I had spent in doing it, and behold, all was vanity and a striving after wind.

from Ecclesiastes 2:4–11

There is an old story about a newly elected politician in Washington, D.C., who was getting oriented to the capital by an elder senator. At one point, the two of them were standing on the banks of the Potomac, when the senator pointed out an old deteriorating log that was floating by. The old-timer remarked, "This city is like that log out there." The fledgling politician asked, "How is that?" The senator came back, "Well, there are probably more than a thousand grubs, ants, bugs and critters on that old log as it floats down the river. And I imagine every one of them thinks that he's steering it."

The story illustrates a key aspect of our human condition—that people continually want to exalt themselves, consider themselves significant, and grasp for greatness. This is portrayed in the story of the Garden of Eden in the fundamental temptation to try to be "like God;" and the desire for self-exaltation is illustrated once again a few chapters later in the story of the Tower of Babel. In that saga, the people seek to exalt themselves by means of a massive tower. They say, "Come, let us build ourselves a city, and a tower with its top in the heavens, and let us make a name for ourselves." (Genesis 11:4) The drive for greatness and glory is age-old; and it can be seen across all facets of human behavior today.

Why do people seek enormous houses and exotic cars and all manner of luxuries, when the more you have, the more you have to maintain and fix and clean? People are driven to seek great possessions not because these things make people happier. It is because they make people feel significant. A person who has a grand house and a grand boat and grand car feels grand. It is all part of the desire for self-exaltation.

Why is it that when people make charitable gifts, they so often want recognition? The gift would do just as much good if no one knew from whence it came. But many people will give generously only if they get their name in a publication or on a brick or on a plaque or, better yet, on the side of a whole building! It is because recognition makes people feel grand; it exalts them in the world.

Why is it that people strive for celebrity, to be "somebody" in the eyes of others? Young people in school want to be popular, people using social media feel uplifted if they have numerous followers, and people love to achieve any sort of notoriety. In reality, you can enjoy life more if you are not in the limelight. But people want the spotlight—again out of the desire for self-exaltation.

But the story of the log in the Potomac—with each bug imagining itself to be captain of the log—illustrates the folly of grasping after greatness. No matter how high and mighty people try to make themselves, in their own eyes or in the eyes of others, the reality is that we are all tiny mortal creatures, who occupy a minute place in a current of time that we do not control.

But human grasping after glory is not only an exercise in folly; it also leads to serious damage to human life. In the story of the Garden of Eden, when Adam and Eve seek to become like God, the result is that they become alienated from God. They subsequently give birth to their sons, Cain and Abel. One day Cain becomes angered because his offering is not acclaimed by God as much as Abel's. Cain cannot stand being a peg lower than his brother Abel, so he attacks and murders Abel. (Genesis 4) The story illustrates how human beings, in the drive to exalt themselves, inevitably fall into envy and hatred, profoundly alienated not only from God but also from one another. This pattern is endlessly repeated throughout the history of the world. The human quest after self-aggrandizement ends with humans becoming not gods, but brutes.

There is a radical contrast to this pattern in the picture of Jesus Christ. The letter to the Philippians puts it this way: "Though he was in the form of God, Christ did not consider equality with God a thing to be grasped, but he emptied himself, taking the form of a servant, being born in human likeness." (Philippians 2:6–7)

Jesus Christ is the reversal of the story of the Garden of Eden. Christ is one with God; but in a precise counter movement to the story of Adam and Eve, Christ does not grasp after that equality with God, but he empties himself and embarks on a path of servanthood, entering the world in human form. Moreover, he enters into the lowliest possible rank in human society! Jesus is born in poverty and is laid for his first night into a feed trough for a crib. He is a member of an oppressed people, and he grows up in obscurity in a small town. He becomes an itinerant preacher in a disdained land; and his life is cut short at a young age through a most ignominious death – crucifixion.

Through it all, Jesus does not seek after any of the elements of greatness that are so sought after in our world today.

The temptation story, reported in detail at the beginning of the gospels of Matthew and Luke[1], shows Jesus explicitly rejecting each major aspect of the common human quest after self-exaltation. He is tempted by material satisfaction ("Turn these stones into bread..."), and he rejects that. He is tempted by fame ("Throw yourself off the pinnacle of the temple, and let the angels hold you up"), and he rejects that. He is tempted by power ("I will give you all the kingdoms of the world"), and he rejects that. He embarks instead into a lifestyle that involves a thoroughgoing reversal of our typical human values.

While human beings seek wealth, Jesus possesses almost nothing; and in his teaching he says, "Blessed are the poor, for theirs is the kingdom of God." (Luke 6:20) While human beings love fame and honor, Jesus continually downplays his miracles, and suggests taking the lowest place at a banquet table. While human beings love power, Jesus says that he came "not to be served but to serve." (Mark 10:45) While human beings are continually attacking one another to try to advance their position, Jesus declares, "Blessed are the peacemakers, for they will be called children of God." (Matthew 5:9) Repeatedly Jesus flips the usual human concept of "getting ahead." In sharp contrast he proclaims, "The first will be last, and the last first." (Matthew 19:30, 20:16)

---

1   See Matthew 4:1–11 and Luke 4:1–12

There is a story in the gospel of Matthew about how "the disciples came to Jesus and asked, 'Who is the greatest in the kingdom of heaven?'" (Matthew 18:1) The disciples had been following Jesus, but their desire for self-exaltation had not changed one bit; they now wanted to know who will be the greatest in God's kingdom! But Jesus called a child and said, "Truly I tell you, unless you change and become like children, you will never enter the kingdom of heaven. Whoever becomes humble like this child is the greatest in the kingdom of heaven." (Matthew 18:2-4) Elsewhere he said, "Those who exalt themselves will be humbled, and those who humble themselves will be exalted." (Matthew 23:12) According to Jesus, it is humility, rather than the drive for self-exaltation, which will enable us to share fully in God's blessing.

This correlates with the truths noted in the previous chapters. If salvation comes to us as a gift of God, which we are to receive in faith, then we need a core attitude of humility in order to recognize our need for God's grace. Still further, if we are to live in authentic goodness, we will be able to express such goodness only when we stop seeking our own exaltation and join in the kind of servanthood modeled in Jesus. Paradoxically, it is in humility that we finally are "exalted"—not into the glories so sought after in the world, but into the joy and meaning of fellowship with God.

The transforming truth that shines through in the life of Jesus is that *lowliness is the path to godliness*. It is through humility that human beings can participate in the real working of God. As Jesus pointed out to James and John, the desire to "sit in glory" gets human beings nowhere. The way to wholeness and fulfillment in life is Jesus' way of humble servanthood.

The humility commended by Jesus does not mean that we demean ourselves or consider ourselves to be of little value. To the contrary, it means that we understand clearly where our worth lies. Our self-worth lies in the fact that God made us in God's image and God claims us for eternity to live as God's children. We therefore do not need to inflate ourselves into some artificial worthiness through vain exercises in self-exaltation. It is God who exalts us as God embraces us with infinite love.

Following Jesus' way of humility frees us from the foolishness that so often has characterized human living. The folly of human gasping after greatness is well stated in Ecclesiastes chapter two, where the writer talks about a massive personal quest after self-glory and finally concludes, "Then I considered all that my hands had done, and the toil I had spent in doing it, and behold, all was vanity and a striving after wind." (Ecclesiastes 2:11) *Striving after wind* well describes a good deal of human behavior, as people reach after a greatness that is without substance. We are freed from such vanity as we enter instead into Jesus' humble path, in which we can share in the simple goodness of God each day.

Humility also frees us from the terribly destructive behavior that has forever accompanied human grasping after greatness. Living in humble servanthood means that we no longer run roughshod over our neighbor or over the environment in the effort to hoist ourselves ever higher.

We are able instead to show the kind of care and compassion for the world exemplified in Jesus. Thus *lowliness is the path to godliness*. This is why Paul in Philippians urges, "Let the same mind be in you that was in Christ Jesus." (Philippians 2:5)

The idea that *lowliness is the path to godliness* completely shakes up the typical values, priorities, and goals by which people live. It is a transforming truth because, once grasped, it reorders life; and it not only dramatically changes the individual, but it can enable the individual to dramatically change the world. The prime example of that is Jesus.

The Point Is Love

Then one of the scribes came, and having heard them reasoning together, perceiving that Jesus had answered them well, asked him, "Which is the first commandment of all?" Jesus answered him, "The first of all the commandments is: 'Hear, O Israel, the Lord our God, the Lord is one. And you shall love the Lord your God with all your heart, with all your soul, with all your mind, and with all your strength.' This is the first commandment. And the second, like it, is this: 'You shall love your neighbor as yourself.' There is no other commandment greater than these." So the scribe said to him, "Well said, Teacher. You have spoken the truth, for there is one God, and there is no other but he. And to love God with all the heart, with all the understanding, with all the soul, and with all the strength, and to love one's neighbor as oneself, is more than all the whole burnt offerings and sacrifices." Now when Jesus saw that he answered wisely, he said to him, "You are not far from the kingdom of God."

Mark 12:28–34

For God so loved the world that he gave his only Son, that whoever believes in him may not perish but may have everlasting life.

John 3:16

When we cry, "Abba! Father!" it is the Spirit bearing witness with our spirit that we are children of God, and if children, then heirs—heirs of God and joint heirs with Christ.

Romans 8:15–17

If you were to ask contemporary Americans what the point of life is, and if they were truly honest with themselves, they would likely answer that the point of life can be summarized in a pair of two-word phrases: "Be happy" and "Be nice." Ask parents what they want for their children, and a great majority will say that their greatest wish for their children is that they will be happy. They also want their children to be nice – to treat other people kindly. The twin goals of "being happy" and "being nice" can be seen in a great deal of the behavior in contemporary society.

From a religious perspective, there is nothing particularly wrong with desiring to be happy or to be nice; but to make these one's highest aims is to have goals that are woefully inadequate. The quest for personal happiness often does not result in real happiness at all; and value of being nice is scarcely enough to make a moral impact on a troubled world.

Jesus was once asked, "What is the greatest commandment?" This was a way of asking, "What is the point of life?" Jesus' answer consisted of a pair of two-word phrases: "Love God" and "Love neighbor." As he said, "You shall love the Lord your God with all your heart, and with all your soul, and with all your mind, and with all your strength," and "You shall love your neighbor as yourself." (Mark 12:30–31)

Jesus puts love at the center. While compassion is a virtue broadly commended in world religions, no other religion puts love in the center in quite the way that Jesus does. Even as Jesus drew upon the foundation of the Hebrew Scriptures, his perspective went well beyond what others had seen. The two "greatest commandments" that Jesus lifted up are both in the Torah. The first is the Shema,[1] the foundational profession of faith in the book of Deuteronomy, which states "Hear, O Israel: The Lord is our God, the Lord is one. And you shall love the Lord your God with all your heart, and with all your soul, and with all your might." (Deuteronomy 6:4–5) The "second greatest commandment" is drawn from the book of Leviticus: "You shall not take vengeance or bear a grudge against any of your people, but you shall love your neighbor as yourself." (Leviticus 19:18) These two "commandments" had been around for centuries. But there were also the "ten commandments" (all different from the "two greatest commandments") and a great many additional commandments by which the people of Israel were living. The unique insight of Jesus was to draw two principles – love God and love neighbor – sharply into focus as the absolute center of the purpose of life. This is transformational.

To grasp the full import of Jesus' teaching, one must understand what he means by the word "love" – a term sloppily used in contemporary English. In the Old Testament form of the two "greatest commandments," the original Hebrew word in each case is *ahav* אָהַב. This word, meaning "love," has the same sort of broad meaning as our English word "love." It includes many forms of showing

---

1   The Hebrew word *shema*, which means "hear," is the first word of this statement; it has come to denote the whole statement.

affection, commitment, and care. Jesus spoke Aramaic and almost certainly used the Aramaic word that corresponds to *ahav*, the word *chav*; but when Jesus' teaching was rendered into Greek, the language of the New Testament, the word chosen to render his meaning was the word *agape* ἀγάπη. This word captures the essence of what Jesus was talking about when he spoke of loving God and loving neighbor.

Koine Greek, the language of the New Testament, had four different basic words for love. *Eros* indicated romantic love, or could also (especially according to Plato) indicate love of beauty. The word is not found in the New Testament, although the concept is present in the discussion of the relationship between husband and wife. *Storge* described family love. The word appears in a couple of derivative forms in the New Testament, where the basic term indicates "showing mutual affection." *Philia* denoted friendship love. It appears in multiple verses in the Scriptures. All three terms describe love that is in some way returned. Lovers, family members, and friends all extend love and receive love back; if the love is not returned, the person slighted may very well stop offering love. *Eros*, *storge*, and *philia* are all extremely valuable and important; but they are found just as much among the wicked as among the righteous. Drug cartel members display erotic love and love their family and their friends, often with great passion.

The fourth kind of love is far more unique. It is the love described with the term *agape*. While the other forms of love are in some ways conditional — expecting love in return — *agape* love is unconditional. It is love given regardless of the response and irrespective of any benefit to be gained. It is the self-giving love that finds its ultimate expression in Jesus.

Agape love is the love by which God loves the world. It is the term for love used in Jesus' statement, "For God so loved the world that he gave his only Son that whoever believes in him might not perish but have everlasting life." (John 3:16) Jesus comes and gives his life for humanity, even though human beings respond with rejection. God continues to love even if we are ignoring or spurning God altogether. In Jesus' two "greatest commandments," he encourages us to put this kind of unconditional, persistent love at the center of our life.

To "love God" in this way means that we love God without concern for reward. This is quite different from the religious practice found generally in ancient near eastern religion. People worshipped the gods because they were looking some benefit, and their attitude toward the gods was not well described by the word "love." They approached the gods in the way that they approached their tyrant rulers—with an obeisance aimed at self-promotion.

Jesus represented a radically different attitude toward God. In calling people to "love God," Jesus moved entirely away from the transactional thinking that had often taken hold in religion—whereby people would engage in religious practice with a view toward receiving something they wanted. Jesus invited people instead into a close, loving relationship. He pictured that relationship with perhaps the most compelling image of unconditional love—the love between a parent and child.

The Hebrew Scriptures in various places had already used the image of "father" as an image for God, but it was not a prominent image. In the entire Old Testament, there are nine times when the word "father" is used for God. The gospels record Jesus referring to God as "father" roughly two hundred times. Jesus called his followers to address God as "Our Father," and he is even recorded using the term "Abba" to address God.[2]

The ancient Hebrew or Aramaic word for "father" was *ab* אָב , actually pronounced *av*. The form "abba" was akin to the English word "dad" or "daddy." It implied a very close, familiar, caring relationship. Early Christians understood that this is the kind of relationship that we can each have with God. As it is said in Romans, "When we cry 'Abba, Father!' it is the Spirit bearing witness with our spirit that we are children of God." (Romans 8:15-16) To "love God" is to respond to God's love for us by sharing in this deep, personal fellowship with God.

Clearly, to love God is much more than simply to believe in God. Loving God involves a personal commitment to God, a joining of one's life to God. It means to have God at the center of one's life.

This loving relationship leads to Jesus' "second greatest commandment" — to love neighbor. Again the word for love here is *agape*. The nature of this love reaches its highest illustration in Jesus, as he repeatedly demonstrated an expansive love for people that many considered unlovely. The people of Jericho were appalled when Jesus reached

---

2   Mark 14:36

out to the despised tax collector Zacchaeus;[3] and people would have recoiled when Jesus touched lepers to heal them.[4] The Pharisees were aghast that Jesus was "eating with tax collectors and sinners;"[5] and the people of Nazareth were so incensed when Jesus suggested that God extends grace to foreigners that they tried to throw him off a cliff.[6] The *agape* love of Jesus showed no bounds. He embraced those condemned by others and loved those hated by others.

In such outreach, Jesus continually gave of himself in compassion without thought for receiving anything in return. His love in every case was a free gift. He lived out the principle that he put forth in his teaching when he said, "If you love those who love you, what credit is that to you? And if you do good to those who are good to you, what credit is that to you? Even sinners do that. But love (*agape*) your enemies..." (Luke 6:32–33,35) Such *agape* love would find its ultimate expression on the cross.

Obviously, this goes vastly beyond all human efforts to "be nice" to other people. Niceness is a social convention that enables people to get along well in society. Niceness makes life more pleasant for everyone, and those who are nice generally receive positive feedback for it. *Agape* love, on the other hand, may very well be costly for the person offering it. It involves giving without reward, and it means including in love some people that others might want to

---

3   Luke 19:1–9
4   Matthew 8:1–3
5   Mark 2:16, Matthew 9:11, Luke 5:30, Luke 15:1–2
6   Luke 4:16–30

exclude. When Jesus offered *agape* love, he engendered a great deal of opposition, and it cost him finally his life.

Inspired by Jesus, people have been moved to demonstrate *agape* love in multiple ways in modern times. *Agape* love was shown by the Freedom Riders in 1961, when they literally risked their lives to win civil rights for others. *Agape* love is shown by volunteers in soup kitchens and clothing centers across the country, who give hours of time to help people they do not know. *Agape* love is shown by people who donate a significant percentage of their income to charity, handing out their hard-earned wealth for the sake of causes beyond themselves. *Agape* love is transformational, as it changes the world at large, and it also changes the people who give it. It entails a reversal of the usual direction of life, so that people become focused not on grasping but on giving.

Jesus called this kind of love the "second" commandment because it springs from the first. When people experience God's unconditional and unlimited love — love poured upon us even though we have not earned it — they are given enormous inspiration to show the same kind of expansive, freely given love to others. As it is said in the first letter of John, "We love because God first loved us." (I John 4:19)

The core insight of Jesus in his "greatest commandments" teaching is that we find the point of life outside of ourselves. This is why those who focus on their own happiness never really get there. It is in reaching beyond ourselves to God and others that we find our true fulfillment. As Jesus said, "Those who seek to save their life will lose it, but those who lose their life for my sake and the gospel's will find it." (Mark 8:35)

The teaching of Jesus also strongly affirms that there **is** a point to life. While some may say that we are in a meaningless universe, Jesus declares quite the opposite. We are here for a reason, and it is to share together in the love of God forever.

You Have a Destiny with God

Mary stood weeping outside the tomb. As she wept, she bent over to look into the tomb; and she saw two angels in white, sitting where the body of Jesus had been lying, one at the head and the other at the feet. They said to her, "Woman, why are you weeping?" She said to them, "They have taken away my Lord, and I do not know where they have laid him." When she had said this, she turned around and saw Jesus standing there, but she did not know that it was Jesus. Jesus said to her, "Woman, why are you weeping? Whom are you looking for?" Supposing him to be the gardener, she said to him, "Sir, if you have carried him away, tell me where you have laid him, and I will take him away." Jesus said to her, "Mary!" She turned and said to him in Hebrew, "Rabbouni!" (which means Teacher). Jesus said to her, "Do not hold on to me, because I have not yet ascended to the Father. But go to my brothers and say to them, 'I am ascending to my Father and your Father, to my God and your God.'"

John 20:11–17

Jesus looked up to heaven and said, "Father, the time has come… You gave your Son authority over everyone so that he could give eternal life to everyone you gave him. This is eternal life: to know You, the only true God…"

John 17:1–3

One of the most commonly held "spiritual ideas" is the idea of heaven. A recent Pew Research study revealed that 72% of Americans believe in heaven, defined as a place "where people who have led good lives are eternally rewarded."[1] The belief in an afterlife has a long history. As best as we can tell, early humans universally had a sense that there is something awaiting us after we die. Ancient burials often included various useful items buried along with the deceased – reflecting a notion that they would need some things for the next life. Ancient societies often venerated ancestors, believing that the ancestors after death continued to exist in some form. These ideas expanded over time, reaching perhaps their most spectacular expression in ancient Egypt. The magnificent burials of the pharaohs and other leading members of Egyptian society involved a massive effort expended toward ensuring that the deceased person would have the best possible path into eternity. The Egyptians developed an elaborate mythology, spelled out in the Egyptian Book of the Dead, which delineated Egyptian speculation about the afterlife.

In this context, there is an astonishing perspective that is reflected in almost the entirety of the Old Testament. Look in the Old Testament for ideas about heaven, and you will find heaven mentioned as the realm of God – the abode where God dwells. But do human beings go to heaven after

---

1   Pew Research Center, Religious Landscape Study, 2014.

death? Start reading in Genesis 1, and continue for chapter after chapter, book after book, and you will find no mention of the idea that people will go to heaven – in almost all of the Old Testament. This is particularly striking given the fact that the Hebrew people had had extensive exposure to Egyptian culture and the elaborate notions of afterlife in Egyptian religion. But to all those ideas, the Old Testament perspective had one basic response: "Hogwash." Mythology about the afterlife was simply rejected. Instead, throughout the Old Testament there is a hesitancy to say much of anything about an afterlife. In what little reference there is to any sort of existence beyond death, Old Testament passages suggest simply that all human beings at death will go to *Sheol*. Sheol, the abode of the dead, was conceived as a misty realm where there is nothing remaining but a faint shadow of what human beings were on earth. As Ecclesiastes puts it, "There is no work or thought or knowledge or wisdom in Sheol, to which you are going" (Eccl. 9:10); or the book of Job says, "As the cloud fades and vanishes, so it is with all who go down to Sheol." (Job 7:9)

Obviously, ancient Hebrew people did not believe in God because they wanted to go to heaven! Religion for them was not a ticket to a nice afterlife. They believed in God because they experienced God as a Reality in life. They sensed God's presence in the world around them, and they encountered God in their journey in life. Their specific beliefs arose not out of speculation but out of what they perceived in their encounter with God. This can be seen throughout the Biblical story. The Biblical narrative is all about God reaching to human beings and revealing

God's self to them. The people formed their religious and moral beliefs in response to that revelation. In the process, the people simply did not perceive any message from God about eternal life, and therefore they did not believe in it.

From a Christian theological perspective, it is quite understandable why people in early Old Testament times would not have received any message from God about eternal life. The Savior had not yet come, and it was centuries before Easter. If the way to eternal life was to be opened through the death and resurrection of Jesus Christ, that way was far from being established. None of this, of course, was on the minds of early Biblical people of faith. What is remarkable is the kind of no-nonsense realism in which they stood. Not given to wishful thinking, they rejected the afterlife ideas so popular among their neighbors. If there was to be anything everlasting about an individual's life, they felt it had to be found in the memory and the legacy that would be carried on by one's descendants.

The Bible has no concept of an immortal soul. In English translations of the Bible, the word "soul" may be used to translate the Hebrew word *nephesh* or the Greek word *psyche*—terms which refer to a person's core spiritual identity. The spiritual nature of human beings consists in all those aspects of what means to be "in the image of God." This may include a God-implanted sense of eternity. But there is no presupposition in the Bible that human beings will themselves continue after death into some kind of eternal existence. The popular contemporary notion that each person is an immortal soul encased within a mortal body is an old Greek idea, not a Biblical one. The Biblical understanding of the human self is akin to the modern scientific understanding—we are unitary beings, whose physical, mental, emotional, and spiritual qualities are all intertwined. At death, the whole self dies. Biblical writings thus hold a very restrained, skeptical attitude toward any fanciful notions about the self floating off into eternity. As the book of Ecclesiastes puts it, "The fate of humans and the fate of animals is the same; as one dies, so dies the other. They all have the same breath, and humans have no advantage over the animals. All go to one place; all are from the dust, and all turn to dust again. Who knows whether the human spirit goes upward and the spirit of animals goes downward to the earth?" (Ecclesiastes 3:19–21) The apostle Paul likewise noted that human beings have a "perishable nature." (I Corinthians 15:53)

The reality of Biblical teaching may come as a surprise to many Americans, who often adopt the widespread notion, assumed to be a Christian idea, that we each have a soul that is inherently immortal. The idea is popular because it plays directly to self-interest. We love to think that we will continue on forever, and we love to imagine our eternity in entirely self-centered terms. People typically envision heaven as a paradise where they will get to do for eternity all the things that they found fun on earth. Heaven becomes an everlasting extension of one's own personal preferences and desires. In this scenario, God is not even particularly necessary. The popular concept is that the soul will automatically continue into its everlasting journey.

This notion is reflected in numerous popular films about heaven. Watch "Heaven Can Wait" or "What Dreams May

Come" or "Soul," and you will see fanciful scenarios which all have the same basic feature—the human soul just naturally continues after death, and God is not really in the picture. These films have their own merits, but they reflect a cultural pattern in which heaven is conceived in self-centered rather than in God-centered terms.

Self-centered fantasies about heaven can have negative ramifications. If heaven is all about me, then this life should also be all about me. Everything is about whether I am achieving my potential and my full enjoyment on my journey. There seems little need to give much thought to God. Such thinking is widespread today. At times, self-centered notions about heaven have had enormously negative results, when people have been moved by eternity myths to do great harm to others. In ancient Egypt, pharaohs pressed countless laborers into grueling service in order to build giant pyramids, not for the glory of God or for the sake the people but for the sake of themselves—because they thought that the grand structure of the pyramid would somehow ensure them a place of everlasting grandeur. At least they made a nice contribution to the future tourist industry! In modern times, self-centered fantasies about heaven have produced an especially horrific result in radical Islamism. The knife or gun wielding terrorist imagines that the slaughter of "infidels" will be the gateway into a personal paradise. Suicide bombing has become the extreme expression of this self-centeredness. In one spectacular explosion, the suicide bomber can give full vent to his or her hate, escape the crummy existence that he or she had on earth, and vault (one imagines) into a heavenly land full of endless pleasures.

The Bible presents a complete reversal from this kind of self-centered thinking. To be centered on the self is what the Bible identifies as the core feature of human sin. In contrast, the Biblical witness is entirely and authentically God-centered. In Old Testament days, people of faith glorified God and celebrated God's greatness without asking the question, "Where is my eternal reward for all this?" In the New Testament, the God-centered witness comes to its peak expression in Jesus Christ, as Jesus' entire life was one of service to God and to God's people.

In the Biblical narrative, the concept of eternal life emerges over time out of this kind of focus upon God. People did not dream up ideas about eternity because they wanted to live forever. They began to sense that God may grant eternal life – out of God's justice and God's love. The belief in God's justice gradually led people to perceive that God will reward good and punish wickedness in a fashion beyond what one sees in this world. The belief in God's love led people to perceive that God will desire to continually hold in love the people that God has created. There thus gradually emerged, by the late Old Testament period, a perception that God – out of God's goodness, justice, and love – might open a way into life everlasting. This was not a belief in any sort of natural immortality; it was a belief that God could create new life beyond death. By the centuries just prior to the birth of Jesus, many Jewish people came to believe that there could indeed be a promise of eternal life for those who have faith.

In the books of Maccabees, which recount the Jewish resistance to extreme persecution by a Greek ruler in the second century B.C., there is an account of the martyrdom of seven brothers. As one is about to die under severe torture, he exclaims to his tormenters, "You dismiss us from this present life, but the King of the universe will raise us up to an everlasting renewal of life." (II Maccabees 7:9) Note that the expectation here is not that people will naturally glide into a nice afterlife. It is that God "will raise up" the faithful to "an everlasting renewal of life."

The Bible never gives a picture of an "immortal soul" that will inevitably keep on living. Eternal life will be possible only if God raises people out of death into life, bringing the mortal self into a dramatically new kind of existence. As the apostle Paul put it, "This perishable body must put on imperishability, and this mortal body must put on immortality." (I Corinthians 15:53) For that to happen, there must be an extraordinarily decisive action by God.

That transformative action unfolds in Jesus Christ. The New Testament declares that Christ on the cross has reconciled sinful humanity with God; and in the resurrection, as Christ is raised from death into life, he opens the way for all humanity into life everlasting. Eternal life thus becomes possible as a gift of God's grace, extended to us through Christ.

The resurrection is also a picture of the nature of the eternal life that God will create. The resurrected Jesus is not a ghost, nor is he a resuscitated body. His form is what Paul would later call a "spiritual body." (I Corinthians 15:44) Although this is beyond our full comprehension, the resurrection conveys four key truths about what eternal life is:

1) Eternal life is real. The risen Jesus is not a figment of people's imaginations. The tomb was actually empty (a fact not even disputed by the enemies of early Christians); and Jesus had concrete encounters with numerous people. They could touch him, and he even ate with them (Matthew 28, Luke 24, John 21). The resurrection establishes the reality of eternal life as a sure promise of God.

2) Eternal life involves the retention of our identity. Jesus after the resurrection is still Jesus. Throughout the centuries, as human beings have speculated about eternity, they have at times imagined that the human "spirit" might change or lose its particular identity over time. In Hinduism, there is the notion of reincarnation, whereby the spirit reenters the world as another person or even an animal. In Buddhism, there is an idea that the "soul" is like a drop of spray from the ocean, which ultimately just blends back into the whole. The Biblical picture is grounded in the proclamation that God created you and values you; eternal life must therefore involve you continuing as you.

3) Eternal life means relationships with God and others. Jesus meets and converses with his followers, and he says, "I am ascending to my Father." (John 20:17) The Biblical picture is that God created us to be in fellowship with God and in community with one

another. These relationships must therefore be a core feature of everlasting life.

4) Eternal life is a gift of God. It is what God makes possible out of God's infinite love for human beings, come to full expression in Christ. As Jesus said, concerning those who have faith, "I give them eternal life." (John 10:28)

The New Testament thus speaks not of "the immortality of the soul" but of "the resurrection of the body." This of course does not mean that God must raise our literal bones out of the dust. People of faith keep in mind the word of the Lord which says, "As the heavens are higher than the earth, so are my ways higher than your ways and my thoughts than your thoughts." (Isaiah 55:9) The precise nature of eternal life must remain well beyond our full understanding. But the image of the resurrection of the body makes clear that eternal life is not a natural birthright; it is a destiny bestowed upon us by the grace of God.

Furthermore, it is clear in Jesus that heaven is far more than the extended personal vacation that many people often fancy it to be. In Jesus' day there was an old Greek idea of the Elysian fields—an eternal realm of pleasant meadows and sunshine and soft breezes, where it was imagined that people who had been good on this earth would bask in luxurious bounty.[2] Popular thinking about heaven today has a great deal in common the Elysian Fields myth, although moderns might envision heaven more as a kind of everlasting Disney World. Whenever people imagine heaven as a perpetual personal playground, however,

2   See Pindar, Odes (2.59–75)

they seldom reflect about whether this imagined heaven would truly be a place of lasting joy. Even an eternal Disney World would surely become boring, and its residents would soon be grumbling about all sorts of inconveniences and fighting with each other about who was cutting in line!

Throughout the Scriptures, there is a consistent message that human beings will find their true fulfillment and joy when they enter into fellowship with God. It makes sense, therefore, that the core feature of heaven is union with God; and this is exactly how Jesus speaks of it. When talking about going to heaven, he says, "I am going to the Father" (John 14:28); and in his "high priestly prayer," the prayer that he offered just prior to his arrest and crucifixion, Jesus said, "This is eternal life: to know You, the only true God." (John 17:3) For Jesus, the essence of heaven is communion with God.

The New Testament picture of heaven is thus entirely God-centered. This picture continues throughout all the books of the New Testament, culminating in the visions of heaven portrayed in the book of Revelation. In the multiple "glimpses of heaven" offered in the course of that book, there are continually images of heavenly beings gathered around God's throne, singing God's praises. Heaven is a realm where God is at the center; and all God's children rejoice as they share in harmony with God.

This whole picture of heaven is revolutionary in the course of human thinking about eternity; and it has a transformative message both for the doubters of heaven and the believers in heaven. For those disinclined to believe in any idea of heaven, the Biblical narrative begins right where they are – denying eternal life. The Biblical word grows cautiously out of an unflinching skepticism about the subject. The ultimate Biblical proclamation – that you have an eternal destiny with God – is based not on wishful thinking but upon clear perceptions of what God is doing. It is thus a compelling witness for those who doubt.

At the same time, for those who wish to believe in heaven, the Bible challenges easy assumptions about eternity and simple fantasies about a personal paradise. It points to the only real hope and fulfillment that human beings have, as it directs people to ground their lives upon God.

Heaven is not a nice place where good people get to go when they die. Heaven is a glorious destiny with God, made possible through God's central saving action in Jesus Christ, which enables even sinners to enter an everlasting loving fellowship with God and with one another. That is a transforming message, because when taken to heart, it shapes how people live in the present, and it provides a solid hope for the future.

The Future Is in God's Hands

No one knows what the future holds; no one can tell what is to come. As no one has power to restrain the wind, no one has power over the time of their death.

Ecclesiastes 8:7–8

Many are the plans in a person's mind, but it is the purpose of the Lord that will stand.

Proverbs 19:21

"Therefore I tell you, do not worry about your life, what you will eat or what you will drink, or about your body, what you will wear. Is not life more than food, and the body more than clothing? Look at the birds of the air; they neither sow nor reap nor gather into barns, and yet your heavenly Father feeds them. Are you not of more value than they? And can any of you by worrying add a single hour to your span of life? And why do you worry about clothing? Consider the lilies of the field, how they grow; they neither toil nor spin, yet I tell you, even Solomon in all his glory was not clothed like one of these. But if God so clothes the grass of the field, which is alive today and tomorrow is thrown into the oven, will he not much more clothe you—you of little faith?

*Therefore do not worry, saying, 'What will we eat?'
or 'What will we drink?' or 'What will we wear?' For
it is the Gentiles who strive for all these things; and
indeed your heavenly Father knows that you need
all these things. But seek first the kingdom of God
and God's righteousness, and all these things will
be given to you as well.*

Matthew 6:25–33

*"Surely I know the plans I have for you," declares
the Lord, "plans for your welfare and not for harm,
to give you a future with hope."*

Jeremiah 29:11

*"I am the Alpha and the Omega," says the Lord God,
"who is and who was and who is to come, the Al-
mighty."*

Revelation 1:8

Religion in every form has had a strong interest in the future. Ancient religious practice often included the use of soothsayers and seers or the consulting of oracles, in order to try to gain insight into what might be coming in the days and years ahead. Ancient religion also often included rituals designed to shape the future – to ensure, for example, the coming of rain and a bountiful harvest. These twin desires – to know the future and to shape the future – have continued strongly among human beings into the present day.

The Biblical narrative displays a very different perspective on the future. Human efforts to predict the future are considered foolish, and all forms of fortunetelling are condemned.[1] The Scriptures do encourage people to act in ways that will have a positive impact on the future; but any effort to determine the future, through magical practices or otherwise, is vain. As it is said in the book of Ecclesiastes, "No one knows what the future holds; no one can tell what is to come. As no one has power to restrain the wind, no one has power over the time of their death." (Ecclesiastes 8:7–8) The future, in the Biblical view, lies in the hands of God.

---

1   "No one shall be found among you who practices divination, or is a soothsayer, or an augur... or who consults ghosts or spirits, or who seeks oracles from the dead." (Deuteronomy 18:10–11)

Moreover, the very nature of time, in the Biblical understanding, is quite different from what people typically thought in ancient religions. Ancient peoples generally had a cyclical view of time. They felt that everything moves in an endless circle, like the seasons of each year. Their interest in the future had to do with trying to know and control what will happen in the next cycle. The Bible, in contrast, has a linear view of time. There is a beginning, there is progress, and there is a destination, and it is all under the sovereign rule and guidance of God. This linear, progressive view of time is evident in the entire unfolding of the Biblical story. The purpose of faith, in this context, is to become rightly joined with how God is moving.

There is a striking connection between this Biblical view of time and the understanding of modern science. The first verse in Genesis states, "In the beginning..." (Genesis 1:1)—declaring that there was a beginning point of the universe. It also says that originally everything was "a dark formless void." (Genesis 1:2) Modern physics also posits that there was a beginning to all things—the big bang—which brought the universe into existence out of a dark formless void. The first chapter of Genesis is not intended to be a science manual; but in its broad poetic strokes, it corresponds in an uncannily close fashion to the scientific description of the origin of the universe. Physicists say that the first thing to emerge from the big bang was light; and this is exactly what the Bible describes in the first moment of creation. On day one God says, "Let there be light." (Genesis 1:3) Science describes the formation of our planet as a progressive process in which the earth takes shape and life forms gradually emerge, culminating with human beings. The same kind of progressive development is portrayed in the "six days of creation" in Genesis. Within this whole process, it is possible to identify the particular point when everything began. Science places the big bang roughly 13.8 billion years ago.

Logically, one can ask the question, "What was before the big bang?" In physics, this an unanswerable and fundamentally nonsensical question, because according to modern physics, time was created with the big bang as a part of the structure of the universe. There is nothing "before" the big bang because there is no time outside of the big bang and its consequences. This understanding reflects the fact that all we can know through science is what we are able to observe in this universe. Yet the human mind is quite capable of looking at that point 13.8 billion years ago and recognizing that there must be something beyond it, something "prior" to it.

The Biblical witness is that it is God who is prior, who is — in the language of Aristotle — the First Cause or Prime Mover. This understanding entails a decisive insight — that God is outside of time. The relationship of God to time is portrayed in notable fashion in the poetry of Genesis. In the description of creation in Genesis 1, God *creates time.* The "days of creation" — the progression of time — appear as a part of God's creative work. Again, there is a remarkable correspondence here to the idea in modern science that time emerges after the big bang.

But the Bible goes beyond what science can see by looking past the universe itself to the Ultimate Reality out of which the universe comes. God, in the Biblical view, is not a part of the universe but is the source and ruler of it all. Therefore God is not bounded by the material laws which God has made or the progression of time which God has established. God is outside of it all.

The relationship of God to the world is thus analogous to the relationship between an author and a book. A book has a beginning, a story line, and a conclusion, all under the sovereignty of the author. From the perspective of the characters in the book, they are all making decisions and engaging in actions from page to page; and from the vantage point of any one page, it is impossible to see ahead. Everything is happening within the time sequence of the book. But the author stands outside the book, unbound by the book's "time," and sees the whole book at once. This provides a very helpful model for understanding the relationship between God's eternity and our time, and it solves many questions about the future that people often have which are otherwise perplexing.

The Bible makes clear in many places that God knows the future; but how can this be? Does this mean that God precisely predicts the future? But how could God predict with certainty when so much depends on human decisions that are always uncertain? Does this perhaps mean that God foreordains the future, predetermining what everyone will do? But in that case human beings would not have freedom, since everything would be fixed. The conundrum is solved with the insight that God is outside of time. God knows the future not by predicting or predestining it, but because God sees the future, just as an author sees the concluding chapters of a book. The future is present to God, as is also the past.

The insight that God is outside of time also solves some of the questions that people often have about eternal life. When the New Testament speaks about what will happen for believers after death, it makes statements that may strike the reader as inconsistent. Some passages suggests that the faithful will be lifted at the moment of death into fellowship with God. As Jesus said to the man next to him on the cross, "Today you will be with me in paradise." (Luke 23:43) Other passages suggest that the faithful will enter into heaven at a "last judgment" in the distant future. As Jesus said at another point, "I will raise them up on the last day." (John 6:54) Which way is it? Do believers enter heaven "today" or on "the last day"? Sometimes Christians have launched into elaborate speculations to try to reconcile these two apparently different notions. But there is no problem at all when one recognizes that God is outside of time. From the standpoint of time, there may be a vast distance between "today" and "the last day"; but those two points are the same moment within God's eternal now.

This also accounts for how the cross of Christ can be an eternally reconciling act. How can Jesus' death atone for your sin, when the crucifixion was two millennia ago, and you were not even born yet? There is also the question about people of faith who lived prior to Jesus. Are they simply lost, because they died before Jesus had atoned for anyone's sin? The answer is provided, once again, in the truth that God is outside of time. From the perspective of God, the moment of Christ offering his life for our salvation is simultaneous with the moment of your life and the moment of the life of Abraham. The atonement of Christ applies to every "page of the book." This is why Jesus could affirm that Abraham, Isaac, and Jacob were alive by the resurrecting power of God.[2]

The Biblical witness thus serves to completely transform how people look toward the future. From our standpoint in time, the future often appears to be completely uncertain and quite threatening. But the transforming truth declared in the Scriptures is that *the future is in the hands of God*. The universe is not simply a random and doomed realm; it is a purposeful creation upheld by the one God who is good, who is leading all things toward a positive destiny. This means that, as Jesus said, we do not need to worry about the future. We can trust instead in the providential care of God. It also means that we do not need to resign ourselves to being in a pointless universe; we can know rather that we are a part of a grand story of a loving Creator, and so we find our own purpose and destiny as we live into the future that God has for us. Grounded in the truth that the future is in God's hands, we are able finally to look into the future with confidence and a sure hope. As the apostle Paul said, "For I am convinced that neither death, nor life … nor things present, nor things to come, nor powers, nor height, nor depth, nor anything else in all creation, will be able to separate us from the love of God in Christ Jesus our Lord." (Romans 8:38–39)

The Biblical story has a beginning, and it has a conclusion; but the conclusion is not an end. It is rather a

2   Mark 12:26–27

fulfillment. It is a joining in the eternity of God's light and love. To take hold of that future is transforming, and it promises a transformation that is everlasting.

Epilogue

Many truths are transformative, but different kinds of truth are transformative in different ways. Scientific truth transforms our understanding of the material world. Because it deals with the physical universe, scientific truth is cumulative. The discoveries of one generation can be carried forward, each generation building on the discoveries of the past, so that there is progress toward new understandings. With scientific truth, the whole human race moves forward with each discovered truth, even when particular individuals do not understand the science at all.

Religious truth transforms our understanding of ourselves – who we are, what our purpose is, how we are to live, how we are to be liberated from all that would pull us down, and what our destiny might be. Because religious truth is personal, it is not cumulative. The truth must be realized afresh by each individual, and spiritual progress must occur within the heart and soul of each person.

As has been noted in this book, there have been watershed moments in the history of religion, when key spiritual truths have been apprehended in new ways by human beings. According to the Biblical witness, the central watershed moment is Jesus Christ. Transformative spiritual truths can shape all of human society; and yet this does not mean that every individual is automatically moved forward to a higher spiritual level than past generations. For spiritual truth to transform an individual, it must be grasped anew by that person.

This is why old science textbooks are obsolete, but Biblical stories and passages are ever current; because when it comes to spiritual and moral truth, every human being in every age confronts the same basic questions and issues and is challenged in the same way. Each person must recognize, respond to, and be changed by God's Truth.

This book has outlined ten transforming truths:

The one God is good
God created you in God's image
The problem is sin
God acts to save
God acts in grace
God leads us into what is right
Lowliness is the path to godliness
The point is love
You have a destiny with God
The future is in God's hands

Taken together, these truths are radically transformative. They change you and me when we embrace them in faith.